Armies of Ancient Italy
753–218 BC

Armies of Ancient Italy
753–218 BC

From the Foundation of Rome to the Start of the Second Punic War

Gabriele Esposito

Pen & Sword
MILITARY

First published in Great Britain in 2020 by
Pen & Sword Military
An imprint of
Pen & Sword Books Ltd
Yorkshire – Philadelphia

Copyright © Gabriele Esposito 2020

ISBN 978 1 52675 185 0

A CIP catalogue record for this book is
available from the British Library.

Typeset by Mac Style
Printed and bound in India by Replika Press Pvt. Ltd.

Pen & Sword Books Limited incorporates the imprints of Atlas, Archaeology,
Aviation, Discovery, Family History, Fiction, History, Maritime, Military, Military
Classics, Politics, Select, Transport, True Crime, Air World, Frontline Publishing,
Leo Cooper, Remember When, Seaforth Publishing, The Praetorian Press,
Wharncliffe Local History, Wharncliffe Transport, Wharncliffe True Crime
and White Owl.

For a complete list of Pen & Sword titles please contact

PEN & SWORD BOOKS LIMITED
47 Church Street, Barnsley, South Yorkshire, S70 2AS, England
E-mail: enquiries@pen–and–sword.co.uk
Website: www.pen–and–sword.co.uk

Or

PEN AND SWORD BOOKS
1950 Lawrence Rd, Havertown, PA 19083, USA
E-mail: Uspen-and-sword@casematepublishers.com
Website: www.penandswordbooks.com

Contents

Gabriele Esposito is a military historian who works as a freelance author and researcher for some of the most important publishing houses in the military history sector. In particular, he is an expert specializing in uniformology: his interests and expertise range from the ancient civilizations to modern post-colonial conflicts. During recent years he has conducted and published several researches on the military history of the Latin American countries, with special attention on the War of the Triple Alliance and the War of the Pacific. He is among the leading experts on the military history of the Italian Wars of Unification and the Spanish Carlist Wars. His books and essays are published on a regular basis by Osprey Publishing, Winged Hussar Publishing and Libreria Editrice Goriziana; he is also the author of numerous military history articles appearing in specialized magazines like *Ancient Warfare Magazine*, *Medieval Warfare Magazine*, *The Armourer*, *History of War*, *Guerres et Histoire*, *Focus Storia* and *Focus Storia Wars*.

Acknowledgements

This book is dedicated to my exceptional parents, Maria Rosaria and Benedetto, for the great love and fundamental support that they continue to give me every day. This present work is much better than it would have been without their precious observations, deriving from long experience.

A very special mention goes to the many re-enactment groups and living history associations that collaborated with their photos to the creation of this book: without their incredible work of research and re-enactment, the final result of this publication would have not been the same. In particular, I want to express my deep gratitude to the following groups/associations: *Antichi Popoli*, *Athenea Prómakhos*, *Confraternita del Leone/Historia Viva*, *Contoutos Atrebates*, *G.A.S.A.C.*, *Hetairoi*, *Les Ambiani*, *Les Mediomatrici*, *Les Trimatrici*, *Teuta Arverni* and *Teuta Osismi*.

Introduction

The main aim of this book is to present a detailed reconstruction of the military history of ancient Italy, dealing with the period 753–218 BC. This long historical phase, which lasted for more than five centuries, saw a series of fundamental political changes in the Italian peninsula; these started to take place in 753 BC when, according to ancient tradition, a great warrior named Romulus – who was reputedly the son of Mars – founded the city of Rome. Generally speaking, the early decades of Roman history have never been as popular and well-studied as those which saw the ascendancy of the Roman Empire or the decline of Roman civilization. This is mostly due to two reasons: firstly, the primary sources that we have to reconstruct early Roman history are very scarce and usually come from later periods (for example, many of them were produced some centuries after the events they describe); secondly, the early centuries of Roman history are full of intricate events that involved many other peoples living throughout the Italian peninsula. It would be a mistake to think that the Romans were the only important civilization of ancient Italy or that they easily became the dominant power of that part of the Mediterranean world. As we will see, the political and military success of Rome was against all odds: much more powerful civilizations, like that of the Etruscans or of the Greeks from southern Italy, could have easily unified Italy before the Romans or defeated them decisively.

In this book we will try to describe the military organization of the Roman state from 753–218 BC, as well as that of all the Italian peoples who were progressively defeated and absorbed by the Romans. Our analysis will end with 218 BC, which was the first year of the Second Punic War: with the decisive defeat of Hannibal and his Carthaginians, Rome finally secured its complete dominance over the whole of the Italian peninsula and could start looking at other areas of the Mediterranean world for further conquest. During five centuries of continuous wars against other Italic peoples, the Romans suffered several defeats and on some occasions their city risked being destroyed; however, Rome was able to gain the upper hand in this long and difficult struggle, mostly thanks to its superior military structures.

The long historical period described in this book can be divided into three great phases: the first, starting in 753 and ending in 509 BC, saw the ascendancy of Rome as the dominant power in the region of Latium; the second period, starting in 509 and ending in 280 BC, marked the transformation of Rome into the leading power of central Italy; the last phase, running from 280–218 BC, saw the Roman conquest of northern and southern Italy. The first phase corresponded to the age during which Rome was a monarchy, and during which the city was ruled by the famous 'Seven Kings': Romulus, Numa Pompilius, Tullus Hostilius, Ancus Marcius, Tarquinius Priscus, Servius Tullius and Tarquinius Superbus. Each of these kings, starting from the founder Romulus, fought wars against the other peoples who lived in the region of Latium. This was one of the most fertile regions of the entire Italian peninsula and was crossed by the River Tiber, on whose southern shore Rome was built. Most of the peoples who inhabited Latium were warlike, used to living in very harsh conditions: as a result, they proved to be deadly enemies for the Romans, who had many difficulties in defeating them. The second historical phase corresponded to the so-called 'early Roman Republic': at the beginning of this new age, the Romans abandoned monarchy as their form of government and transformed their city into a republic, guided by two consuls and an assembly of nobles known as the Senate. During this period of its history, Rome had to fight some terrible wars against those Italic peoples who dominated the central part of Italy. Most notably, the Romans had to confront the Etruscans and the Samnites: the first had the most advanced civilization of ancient Italy, while the latter were the fiercest warriors of the entire peninsula. After defeating them, the Romans obtained control of central Italy and could enter the next phase of their expansionism, which saw them fighting against the Celtic tribes of northern Italy and the Greek colonies of southern Italy. By 218 BC, the marginal areas of the peninsula were also in Roman hands and Italy was finally unified under a single power.

Chapter 1

The Foundation of Rome and the Army of the Early Kings

Before trying to reconstruct how Rome was born and why such a city was founded, we should describe the geographical context of Latium. This region of central Italy was divided into two main parts, one located north of the Tiber and the other south of the river. The northern part was in the Etruscan sphere of influence, while the southern one – known as 'Latium Vetus', or 'Old Latium' – was inhabited by several different peoples. Around 753 bc, the Tiber was an extremely important means of communication, connecting the inland valleys of central Italy with the Mediterranean Sea. The peoples of central Italy, especially those living in the Apennine mountains, extracted great quantities of salt from their territories and used the Tiber to transport them to the sea; at the mouth of the river, the Italic merchants exchanged their salt – which was of excellent quality – with Phoenician or Greek traders for artefacts like vases. Whoever controlled the mouth of the Tiber also controlled the commercial exchanges taking place between central Italy and the Mediterranean world; Rome was built at this highly strategic part of Latium. The location had many positive features: it was not far from the sea and comprised seven hills, which were easily defensible in case of foreign attack. The coastal area of Latium was mostly covered by unhealthy marshes, where it was impossible to live or build a city. Only the area of the 'Seven Hills' could be inhabited by a large community. Due to all these positive features, the site where Rome was built had already been occupied, with two small settlements built in the area, one by the Etruscans and another by the Sabines (one of the peoples living in the Latium Vetus). These two settlements were not proper villages but merely small commercial outposts, whose main function was to control the mouth of the Tiber.

The 'Seven Hills' were all located south of the river, where the course of the Tiber was narrowed by the presence of a small island known as 'Isola Tiberina'. This island represented the most important ford of the Tiber, and was thus used on a regular basis to connect northern and southern Latium, being part of an important land route that was mostly used to move cattle around the region. The geographical site of the 'Seven Hills' was at the centre of two important commercial routes: one connecting the interior regions of central Italy with the sea and the other connecting the Etruscan territories of Tuscany and northern Latium with the Greek colonies of southern Italy.

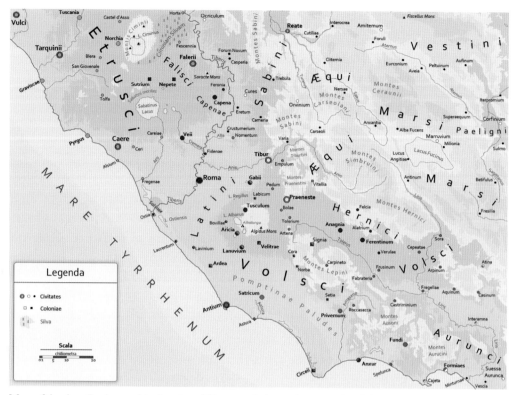

Map of Ancient Latium, with the city of Rome and the various peoples living in the region: Etruscans (north of the Tiber), Latins, Sabines, Equi, Volsci and Marsi. (*CC BY-SA 3.0, Wikimedia User ColdEel and Ahenobarbus*)

Around 753 BC, a new community guided by a warrior leader arrived in the 'Seven Hills' area and built a small village. This new settlement gradually became strong enough to absorb the earlier two centres founded by the Etruscans and Sabines, thus forming a new city that would become known as Rome.

But who were this new community and its warrior leader, and why did they came to the 'Seven Hills'? According to tradition, the warrior leader who founded the new city and provided its name was Romulus, son of Mars and Rhea Silvia, the daughter of King Numitor of Alba Longa. We need to go back to a previous mythical tradition to understand who Numitor was and the importance of Alba Longa. According to ancient tales which were reported by Virgil in his *Aeneid*, after the end of the Trojan War the hero Aeneas landed on the coast of Latium at the head of a band of Trojan survivors who were searching for a new land to live in peace. Once in Italy, Aeneas had to fight a bloody war against the local peoples of the Latium Vetus in order to conquer territory for his community. At the end of the conflict, the Trojans were permitted to remain in Italy and merged with the Latins, the most important people of Latium.

The son of Aeneas, Julo, later founded a city known as Alba Longa that soon became the most important urban centre of the Latium Vetus. Julo's royal family continued to reign over Alba Longa for decades, eventually leading to Numitor taking the throne. However, Numitor was deposed by his brother Amulius, who usurped power in the

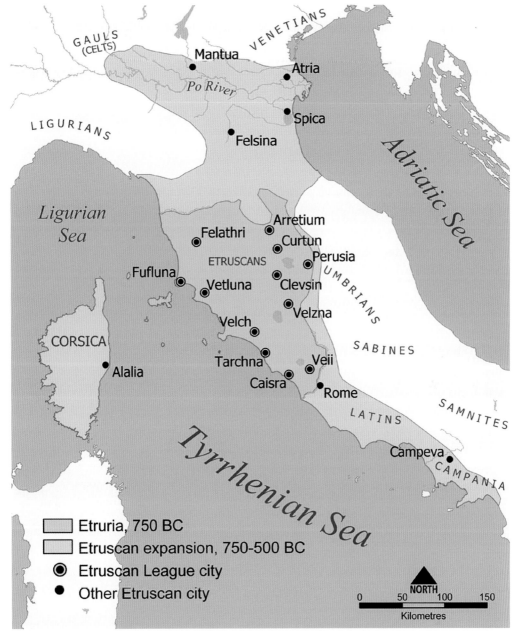

Map of Etruria, showing the twelve main cities of the Etruscan League (the *Dodecapoli*). (*CC BY-SA 3.0, Wikimedia User NormanEinstein*)

city. Rhea Silvia, daughter of Numitor, was obliged by Amulius to become one of the Vestal Virgins (sacred priestesses) so that she could not have any male heir who could claim the throne of the city as legitimate heir of Numitor.

Amulius' plans, however, came to nothing, for despite becoming a Vestal Virgin, Rhea Silvia gave birth to two male twins who – according to legend – were sons of Mars. Amulius considered the boys, named Romulus and Remus, as potential rivals, so ordered one of his serfs to kill them. For some reason, however, the serf did not kill the twins, instead abandoning them on the banks of the Tiber. Here they were said to have been found by a she-wolf, who took care of them until a local herdsman named Faustulus came across the twins and decided to take them as his own sons. Several years later, the adult Romulus and Remus became aware of their royal origins and decided to join the civil war that was taking place in Alba Longa between the supporters of Amulius and those of Numitor. Thanks to the decisive help of the warrior twins, Numitor was able to regain his throne and defeat the usurper Amulius. Romulus and Remus, wishing to become kings of their own city, then decided to abandon Alba Longa at the head of those herdsmen and shepherds who had fought on their side during the civil war. They returned to the place where they had been found by the she-wolf, on the banks of the Tiber, and decided to found a new city. At this point a heated dispute broke out between the brothers, both of whom wished to be sole king. Remus was killed by Romulus during a duel, and the victor thus became the first monarch of the city.

Romulus soon started to expand his small settlement, attracting an increasing number of Latins who lived in the countryside but saw an opportunity for social improvement in the foundation of a new commercial centre on the Tiber. The Roman king established an asylum for fugitives on one of his hills, where every free man or slave from the nearby villages would receive protection and claim Roman citizenship. Romulus also soon attacked the Sabine settlement in the 'Seven Hills' in order to conquer it. This war, waged against the Sabine king Titus Tatius, later gave birth to the famous legend of the 'Rape of the Sabine Women', according to which the Romans had to kidnap Sabine women in order to generate heirs and thus secure the future of their new city. In reality, this early war of Rome against the Sabines should be interpreted as an attempt by the Sabines to expel Romulus' community from the 'Seven Hills', especially as it saw the participation of several Latin warriors on the side of the Sabines. However, the Romans were able to overcome the Sabines and thus secure their presence at the mouth of the Tiber. Sometime later, they were also able to absorb the Etruscan village located in the 'Seven Hills', but with more peaceful methods.

After defeating the Sabines and Latins, Romulus could finally provide a proper social and military organization for his new city. The population of the city was

Romano-Etruscan hoplite of the First Class, with Montefortino helmet and linen cuirass. (*Photo and copyright by Antichi Popoli*)

divided into three groups or 'tribes', corresponding to the ethnic background of all the new 'Romans': the Ramnes, the Tities and the Luceres. The Ramnes were the Latins who had followed Romulus from Alba Longa, while the Tities were the Sabines of Titus Tatius and the Luceres the Etruscans who had been absorbed peacefully. As a result, we can say that early Rome was a multicultural urban centre where three different ethnic groups lived together with the objective of becoming rich through river trade. Each of the three tribes was divided by Romulus into ten *curia*, or wards. Each tribe was guided by a public official known as a 'tribune', while each *curia* was guided by a *curio*. Each ward was assigned a portion of land and had to pay taxes for its possession. Romulus also chose 100 men from the most prominent families of his new city and grouped them into an assembly known as the Senate. These men were called *patres* ('fathers'), and thus the members of their social class – the aristocracy – became known as patricians. The rest of the population made up the plebeians, who were controlled by the aristocrats thanks to a series of social and economic ties. In practice, 100 families (known as *gentes*) controlled the political life of the state: all the poor citizens were simply *clientes* ('clients') of the leading aristocrats.

Each *curia* was to provide 100 infantrymen and ten cavalrymen in time of war; the 100 foot soldiers of each ward made up a *centuria*, the basic military unit of the early Roman Army. Each tribe was made up of ten wards, and thus could provide a total of 1,000 infantry and 100 cavalry. The whole Roman Army could field a total of 3,000 infantrymen and 300 cavalrymen, who were all assembled into a single 'legion' in time of war. Apparently, during these early Roman times the term 'legion' was used to indicate the whole army, and not only a portion of it; this would change only with the creation of the Roman Republic, when the army was divided into two parts and each of the two ruling consuls received command of one legion.

According to contemporary sources, the 300 cavalrymen of the early Roman Army made up a sort of royal guard that had as its main function that of protecting Romulus. Unlike the 3,000 infantry, the 300 horsemen were professional soldiers who came from the richest families of Roman society. Thanks to their superior economic capabilities, they were able to maintain a horse and thus serve as professional fighters. The infantrymen, instead, were probably called to serve only in time of war. The cavalry, known as *celeres*, were the only standing army of early Rome: for this reason they could be considered an elite, as made clear by their name, which meant 'the swift'. It would be wrong, however, to think that they were a cavalry corps in the more modern sense of the word, as they used horses only to move around on the battlefield, not to charge the enemy. The *celeres* were a sort of mounted infantry, who could move much more rapidly than the foot *centuriae* and travel long distances in a relatively short time. Once on the battlefield, however, the Roman cavalry dismounted to fight as normal

Romano–Etruscan hoplite, with full personal equipment. (*Photo and copyright by Antichi Popoli*)

Romano–Etruscan hoplite with round shield, decorated with a typical Etruscan emblem. (*Photo and copyright by Antichi Popoli*)

infantrymen. Obviously, thanks to their social background, they had the best personal equipment and underwent some sort of professional training that marked them out as a chosen force.

During his thirty-seven years of rule, Romulus conducted several wars against the peoples whose territories bordered with that of Rome. As we have already seen, his first major war was that fought against the Sabines of Titus Tatius. The outcome of this conflict was decided by the Battle of Lacus Curtius, during which, according to legend, the Sabine women intervened in order to stop the fight between their Sabine fathers and their new Roman husbands. The clash, in fact, was the direct result of the 'Rape of the Sabine Women'. We can consider the Battle of Lacus Curtius as an attempt by the Sabines to stop Roman expansionism in the 'Seven Hills' region. What we know for sure is that the Romans had great difficulties during the encounter, since the Sabines had a more numerous and well-organized army. By the time of the battle, Romulus had not yet properly organized his military forces, and thus he had to augment his warriors by using any possible method. As well as asking for help from his grandfather Numitor, who sent him an auxiliary contingent of soldiers from Alba Longa, he also recruited a number of Etruscan mercenaries, who were under the command of Lucumo (one of his personal friends). We know very little about the Battle of Lacus Curtius, but it is probable that it ended in a stalemate. At the end of the clash, a peace treaty was agreed between the opposing sides, according to which the Romans of Romulus and the Sabines of Titus Tatius would form a single people. Apparently, the two kings ruled jointly for several years until the Sabine monarch died.

During the later years of his life, Romulus conducted several campaigns against the Etruscan settlements located north of the Tiber. The most important of these was Veii, which had the same expansionist ambitions as Rome and wanted to exert economic control over the mouth of the river. Romulus ravaged the countryside of Veii, but was never able to conquer the city due to the impressive walls that had been built by the Etruscans. The Roman king, however, was able to occupy the smaller Etruscan settlement of Fidenae, that was located a few miles north of Rome along the course of the Tiber. When Romulus died in 717 BC, the Roman presence in Latium was thus already quite strong. The new city connected the Etruscan world of the north with the various peoples of the Latium Vetus. Romulus was succeeded as king by Numa Pompilius, a Sabine noble. It should be noted that until the creation of the Republic, the three ethnic components of Rome remained quite distinct and thus selected their kings by a principle of alternation: Numa Pompilius was Sabine, Tullus Hostilius was Latin, Ancus Marcius was Sabine and the last three monarchs were all Etruscans.

Numa Pompilius, who had married the only daughter of Titus Tatius, spent most of his long reign organizing the Roman state from a religious and social point of view.

Romano–Etruscan hoplite of the First Class, with Corinthian helmet and composite cuirass (made of linen and bronze scales). (*Photo and copyright by Confraternita del Leone / Historia Viva*)

According to tradition he did not fight a single war, but what we can say for sure is that he was able to maintain peace between Rome and the Sabines during the turbulent years that followed the death of Romulus. In 673 BC, Tullus Hostilius became king of Rome and soon started a new foreign policy. After decades of relative peace, he decided to attack most of the peoples living around his city, notably the Latins of Alba Longa. As we have seen, Alba Longa was the most important centre in the Latium Vetus, and when Rome was founded the inhabitants of Alba Longa already exerted an indirect leadership over most of the other Latin communities. Tullus Hostilius wanted to change all this, since he intended transforming Rome into the leading city of a new Latin Confederation that would comprise all the Latin communities. Obviously Alba Longa could not accept this, and war broke out between the two cities. After decades of military inferiority, by now the Romans were able to face their rivals on almost equal terms, and it became clear that the new war would be a long one. During the following years neither side was able to gain the upper hand in the conflict and both cities suffered great losses. At one point, according to legend, the kings of Rome and Alba Longa arranged a duel between champions to decide the outcome of the war. Each city was to choose three champions from among the ranks of the army; these three, according to what had been suggested by an oracle, were to be brothers. The Roman champions were the Orazi, while those chosen by the king of Alba Long were the Curiazi. After fierce fighting that resulted in the death of three Curiazi and two Orazi, the Romans prevailed. Alba Longa submitted to Rome and agreed to become a vassal of their neighbour.

After this success, Tullus Hostilius turned his attention towards the Etruscan cities of Veii and Fidenae, the latter having revolted against the Romans with the decisive support of Veii. The Roman army marched against the Etruscans to fight a pitched battle, but at the decisive moment of the campaign the king of Alba Longa decided to infringe his pact with Tullus Hostilius and refused to aid the Romans by sending his forces. The Romans thus marched alone against the Etruscans, but still defeated them, after which they moved against the city of Alba Longa and razed it to the ground. The inhabitants of the defeated city were deported to Rome, together with all their goods. In the following years Tullus Hostilius continued to fight against the Etruscans of Fidenae, as well as against the Sabines and Latins (who had been outraged by the destruction of Alba Longa). When Tullus Hostilius died in 641 BC, all these ongoing conflicts were inherited by his successor, Ancus Marcius.

Ancus Marcius was a grandson of Numa Pompilius, but unlike the previous Sabine Roman monarch he had to spend most of his reign on the field of battle. He conducted several indecisive campaigns against the Latins and Sabines. The latter, in particular, had started to raid Roman territory frequently, which caused great damage to the

Romano-Etruscan hoplite of the First Class, with Corinthian helmet and bronze 'muscle' cuirass. The sword is of the Greek *kopis* model. (*Photo and copyright by Confraternita del Leone / Historia Viva*)

Romans. Ancus Marcius was able to stop the enemy raids, but could not decisively defeat the Sabines. The new king did, however, achieve some great military successes against the Etruscans of Veii and Fidenae, with Fidenae conquered and sacked by the Roman army. Ancus Marcius died in 616 BC, after having adopted a young Etruscan aristocrat from the city of Tarquinia as his son during the last years of his life. The youth was named Tarquinius Priscus and became the fifth king of Rome. The presence of an Etruscan noble on the throne of Rome was probably the result of some important political changes that took place around 620–610 BC. Around that time, the Etruscans started to expand themselves south of the Tiber with the objective of annexing Latium Vetus to their already extensive dominions. Tarquinia, one of the largest Etruscan cities, was the main force behind this expansionist process. It is thus highly probable that Rome also came under the Etruscan sphere of influence during this period, or that the Etruscan community in Rome started to exert its dominance over the other two ethnic components of Roman society. In any case, it was under Tarquinius Priscus that the Etruscans of Rome became increasingly rich and numerous, gaining control over the political life of their city.

Chapter 2

The Military Reforms and Campaigns
of the Etruscan Kings

By the time Tarquinius Priscus became king of Rome, the Etruscan cities of Tuscany and northern Latium had already adopted the hoplite military system invented by the Greeks and based on the existence of the citizen-soldier. In Rome, however, the army was still organized according to the structure that had been introduced by Romulus several decades before. Being under the political influence of the Etruscans, the Romans gradually started to adopt the hoplite system and thus their military forces underwent a period of radical change, initiated under Tarquinius Priscus. The use of the new military system was also determined by other factors, such as the arrival of new populations in the territory of Latium Vetus. These were the Equi and Volsci, two warlike peoples who belonged to the larger ethnic group of the Oscans and who arrived in central Italy in search of new fertile lands where they could settle. The Equi established themselves north-east of Rome in a large territory mostly covered by the Apennine mountains that they shared with the Sabines, while the Volsci settled south-west of Rome in land that was largely covered by swamps. Soon after arriving in the Latium Vetus, both the Equi and Volsci started to launch frequent incursions against Roman territory and even menaced the city of Rome. As a result, the Romans had to learn how to fight against these new enemies, who were used to hit-and-run tactics. Tarquinius Priscus initiated a new season of reforms for the Roman Army by doubling the size of his cavalry, which was expanded to 600 men (six *centuriae*). This expansion was made possible thanks to the arrival of many new aristocrats, such as Tarquinius Priscus, in the city of Rome. These men had become rich through commerce and were transforming themselves into an increasingly important component of Roman society. Since military service as *celeres* was seen as a status symbol, these new nobles of Rome wished to serve as cavalrymen like the old aristocrats of the early *gentes*. With the creation of these new mounted *centuriae*, all the Roman cavalry units received a new name: the old ones became known as *Ramnes primi*, *Tities primi* and *Luceres primi*, with the new units named the *Ramnes secundi*, *Tities secundi* and *Luceres secundi*.

The decision to expand his permanent cavalry troops was apparently taken by Tarquinius Priscus after he had to face a massive attack launched by the Sabines. The Romans had been taken by surprise and were only able to repulse their enemies after

Romano–Etruscan hoplite of the First Class, with Chalcidian helmet and *linothorax* (linen cuirass). (*Photo and copyright by Antichi Popoli*)

fighting in the streets of the city. After expanding the cavalry, the new king fought several campaigns against the Latins and was able to conquer some new territories. At this point the Latins decided to form a military alliance with the Etruscans in a bid to stop Roman expansion towards their territories. Several Etruscan cities, but not including Tarquinia, sent their troops to the Latium Vetus in order to take part in what was essentially a civil war of the Etruscan world. Despite their numerical inferiority, the Romans were able to prevail on several occasions and obliged the Latins to abandon their coalition with the Etruscans. The war, however, continued because the Sabines decided to join the Etruscans in their struggle against Rome. After defeating a combined enemy army at Fidenae, the Romans were able to conclude a peace agreement with the Sabines. Yet the Etruscans, guided by the city of Veii, continued the fight against Rome and placed a garrison in Fidenae. After achieving another major victory over the Etruscans, Tarquinius Priscus could finally make peace with his enemies. Rome had been able to stop the expansionism of Veii towards the Latium Vetus and thus retain its supremacy over the Latin world. In 578 BC, Tarquinius Priscus was assassinated by one of Ancus Marcius' sons, who considered the Etruscan king a usurper and who hoped to become king after killing the adopted son of his father. The plot, however, did not work out due to the decisive intervention of Tarquinius Priscus' wife Tanaquil, who had her son-in-law Servius Tullius elected as king.

The new monarch soon initiated a complete reform of the Roman Army, based on a simple principle that all male citizens had to serve in the military structures of the state, according to their economic capabilities. As a result, all the citizens of Rome were divided into three groups according to their census: the aristocracy of the *gentes*, the middle-class of the *adsidui* and the lower-class of the *proletarii*. The aristocrats were those citizens who were rich enough to serve as cavalrymen; the *adsidui* those who could afford to buy the personal equipment of an infantryman; and the *proletarii* those who were too poor to buy any piece of military equipment and who had nothing except their sons and daughters (the *prole*). According to the new Servian military system, political representation was strongly linked to military service. The aristocrats, being able to serve as elite soldiers, could be elected to all the public offices of the state. The *adsidui*, through serving as infantrymen, had the right to vote and choose the public officials. However, the *proletarii*, being unable to provide any military contribution, could not vote and thus had no political representation. The *proletarii* could be called to serve only in case of military emergencies and were to receive their weapons from the state only for the duration of the military campaign in which they were required to take part.

As a result of the Servian reforms, the soldiers of the Roman Army started to be divided into different categories according to their census and not according to their

Romano-Etruscan hoplite with round shield, painted with a distinctive Etruscan emblem. (*Photo and copyright by Antichi Popoli*)

Romano–Etruscan hoplite wearing his helmet. As is clear from this photograph, since the times of the Servian Reforms the heavy infantry of the Roman and Etruscan armies looked very similar to the Greek hoplites. (*Photo and copyright by Antichi Popoli*)

ethnic background or tribe. Around 570 BC, the hoplite military system and the tactical formation known as the phalanx were introduced in Rome, together with the new organizational system based on the census. As a result, each category of soldiers had a different kind of personal equipment and a different tactical function. Basically, the Roman Army was to comprise five classes (or categories) of troops, the first of which included both cavalry and heavy infantry, while the other four were infantry with different kinds of equipment. The cavalry of the First Class was organized on eighteen *centuriae*, for a total of 1,800 mounted aristocrats. Servius Tullius, in fact, added twelve units of horsemen to the six existing ones and thus greatly expanded the general establishment of the Roman cavalry. This is a clear sign of how the aristocratic groups living in Rome were expanding very rapidly, mostly thanks to commerce. A good number of these 'new' nobles were Etruscans who had established themselves in Rome after the city started to be ruled by Etruscan kings. The infantry of the First Class was organized on eighty *centuriae*, for a total of 8,000 hoplites. Half of the eighty *centuriae* were known as *seniores*, while the other forty were known as *iuniores*: the *seniores* units comprised veteran soldiers aged over 46, while the *iuniores* ones were made up by younger men aged between 17 and 46. In practice, the *iuniores* were active units, which could be called to serve in case of war, while the *seniores* were a sort of national reserve that could be called to serve only in case of military emergencies, such as a foreign invasion. To be a member of the First Class, a Roman citizen was required to have an income of 100,000 *assi* (the Roman currency of the time). This would enable him to acquire the typical hoplite equipment of this class: helmet, cuirass, greaves, round shield, spear and sword.

The infantry of the Second Class was organized on twenty *centuriae*, for a total of 2,000 medium infantrymen. Half of the twenty *centuriae* were of *seniores* soldiers, while the other ten were of *iuniores*. To be a member of the Second Class, a Roman citizen needed to have an income of 75,000–100,000 *assi*; the specific equipment of this class included helmet, greaves, rectangular shield, spear and sword. The infantry of the Third Class was organized on twenty *centuriae*, for a total of 2,000 medium infantry. Half of the *centuriae* were of *seniores*, while the other ten were of iuniores soldiers. To be a member of the Third Class, a Roman citizen required an income of 50,000–75,000 *assi*; the equipment of this class included helmet, rectangular shield, spear and sword. The infantrymen of the first three classes, all being equipped with shields, were trained to fight in close order and thus underwent the specific training that was typical of the hoplite formations of the time. The infantry of the Fourth Class was organized on twenty *centuriae*, for a total of 2,000 light infantry. Half of the twenty *centuriae* were of *seniores* soldiers, while the other ten were of *iuniores*. To be a member of the Fourth Class, a Roman citizen was to have an income of 25,000–50,000

Rear view of a *linothorax* worn by a Romano-Etruscan hoplite. (*Photo and copyright by Antichi Popoli*)

assi, to purchase a rectangular shield, spear, sword and javelins. The infantry of the Fifth Class was organized on thirty *centuriae*, for a total of 3,000 light infantrymen. Half of the thirty *centuriae* were of *seniores*, the other fifteen being *iuniores* soldiers. To be a member of the Fifth Class, a Roman citizen was to have an income of 11,000–25,000 *assi*; the equipment of this class included just a sling or some javelins. As is clear from the above, the members of the Fourth Class were essentially specialized light infantrymen, while those of the Fifth Class were simple skirmishers who could harass the enemy with their missile weapons during the initial or final phases of a battle.

In addition to the above, there were also some *centuriae* of specialist troops: two *centuriae* of engineers (known as *fabri*) that were attached to the First Class and two of musicians that were attached to the Fifth Class. The first unit of musicians was made up of *tubicines* who played a tuba, while the second comprised *cornicines* who played a horn. Finally, there was also a 'cadre unit' of 100 *proletarii*: this did not have weapons and could be activated/expanded only in case of military emergency (when it was also necessary to mobilize and equip some numbers of *proletarii*). This peculiar unit was known as *immunis* militia since it comprised men who were formally exempt from any form of military service.

The Roman Army was formally structured on two legions: one was made up by all the *centuriae* of *seniores*, and the other by all the *iuniores*. The senior legion was a sort of reserve corps, while the junior one was the proper 'active army'. The *seniores* legion usually remained on garrison in the city, while the *iuniores* unit marched outside the walls to fight in the open field against the enemy. In total, according to the reform of Servius Tullius, the Roman Army on campaign could field 19,300 soldiers organized in the following units: eighteen *centuriae* of cavalry, 170 *centuriae* of infantry, two *centuriae* of engineers, two *centuriae* of military musicians and one cadre corps of *proletarii*. In general, the Roman Army of this period was not very flexible from a tactical point of view. On the battlefield it needed a lot of space to deploy the whole phalanx made up by the first three classes, and this greatly limited the mobility of the foot troops. The cavalry continued to be a sort of mounted infantry and was usually deployed on the flanks of the phalanx in order to protect it from enemy attacks.

Thanks to his new army, Servius Tullius was able to conduct a series of victorious campaigns against the Sabines and Etruscans, the latter not having recognized him as the legitimate monarch of Rome because of his unorthodox ascendancy to the throne. Three Etruscan cities deployed their armies against Rome: Veii, Caere and Tarquinia. Veii had always been an enemy of Rome, since it had the same ambitions of dominance over the mouth of the Tiber. Caere was gradually becoming one of the richest and largest Etruscan centres, while Tarquinia wanted to have one of its aristocrats on the throne of Rome, as it had until the death of Tarquinius Priscus. The wars fought by

Servius Tullius were long and difficult for the Romans, who had to face the best Etruscan armies of the time. After some victories and several defeats, Rome signed new peace treaties with the Etruscan cities and the power of Servius Tullius was finally recognized as legitimate. By 540 BC, Rome was a rich and ambitious urban centre with a strong dominance over the central part of Latium. Servius Tullius' reign had been an extremely positive one from many points of view, especially the social and military ones. We should not forget, in addition, that it was during his reign that the famous Servian Walls were built in order to protect Rome from enemy assaults. Although the city was by now quite large, it could still have been besieged by a coalition force sent by the Etruscans or the Latins.

Early version of a Corinthian helmet, painted in red. The Roman and Etruscan hoplites employed the same models of helmet that were used by their Greek equivalents. (*Photo and copyright by Athenea Prómakhos*)

In 539 BC, after having completely transformed Rome since his ascendancy to the throne, Servius Tullius was assassinated by another Etruscan who lived in Rome, Tarquinius Superbus. Superbus was the son of Tarquinius Priscus and had married two daughters of Servius Tullius; as a result, he would have probably obtained the Roman throne upon the death of the old king, but in 539 BC he decided that the time had come for him to assume power and the assassination of Servius Tullius was organized. From the outset, Tarquinius Superbus was perceived as a tyrant by the majority of the Roman population because of the circumstances of his ascendancy to the throne and his personality. The new king was extremely ambitious and violent. Differently from Servius Tullius, Tarquinius Superbus did not consider war as one of the options to expand Rome but as the only possible choice. As a result, the new monarch spent most of his reign fighting against the enemies of Rome. Tarquinius Superbus became king without the formal approval of the Senate and the people; in addition, considering Servius Tullius a usurper, he did not permit the body of the dead monarch to be buried. All these acts were perceived as extremely negative by the Romans, who feared that Tarquinius Superbus could become a tyrant

Illyrian helmet with decorated cheek-pieces. This model of helmet was quite popular among the Roman/ Etruscan/Latin hoplites, but also among the Apulian warriors (who were of Illyrian stock). (*Photo and copyright by Athenea Prómakhos*)

like those who ruled many Greek cities at that time (like Syracuse in Sicily, which was the most important Greek city in Italy). In practice, the Romans understood that their monarchy was going to become an absolute one. This became clear when Tarquinius Superbus contracted a large force of Etruscan mercenaries and installed them in Rome to act as his personal royal guard and to suppress any revolts launched by the population. After securing his control over Rome, the new monarch used the excellent military forces inherited from Servius Tullius to attack most of the peoples living in Latium. It was during Tarquinius' reign, for example, that the Romans fought their first war against the Volsci, who were becoming a serious problem for the inhabitants of Latium due to their warlike nature and expansionist ambitions.

As we have already said, the Volsci were newcomers in Latium, having migrated to that area of Italy only recently, together with their 'cousins' the Equi. Both these peoples were of Oscan stock, like the Sabines and the Samnites. The Oscans, as we will see, were a group of peoples with a series of common features. First of all, the Oscan peoples mostly lived on the Apennine mountains, which run down the Italian peninsula from the north (where they are linked with the Alps) to the south (where they reach Sicily) and are characterized by a very harsh climate, especially during winter. As a result, the Oscan peoples were used to a very simple lifestyle and could survive with very little resources in every climatic condition. They did not practice agriculture on a large scale and were mostly shepherds, but over time they learned how to trade with the other peoples and to produce weapons and working tools of good quality. The Equi and Volsci installed themselves on mountainous areas that had not been occupied by other peoples like the Latins or Etruscans. Compared to the Etruscans they had an inferior level of civilization, but were quite numerous and extremely warlike. In addition, the hoplite military system based on the phalanx that was employed by the Latins and Etruscans was of very little use against the Oscan warriors, who did not fight in close order and preferred to conduct guerrilla operations with hit-and-run tactics.

According to contemporary sources, the first war between Rome and the Equi took place under Tarquinius Priscus and ended with a Roman victory, but was just the first step in a struggle that would last for two centuries. The first Roman campaign against the Volsci was organized by Tarquinius Superbus, which resulted in a victory for the tyrant/king but did not cause serious losses to the Volsci. As we will see, the Equi and Volsci would prove to be the deadliest enemies of the early Roman Republic during

Chalcidian helmet with decorated cheek-pieces. Greek helmets were extremely popular in the Italian peninsula, and were also used on a large scale by the Oscan peoples who did not include hoplites in their armies. (*Photo and copyright by Athenea Prómakhos*)

the following decades and would cause serious problems for the Roman military forces. After obtaining his victory over the Volsci, Tarquinius Superbus moved with his army against the Latin city of Ardea, which was one of the most ancient cities of Latium Vetus and one of Rome's traditional rivals. When the king marched on Ardea, the Senate and the people of Rome saw an opportunity to destroy the power of the tyrant and thus decided to revolt. The mercenaries that had been left to garrison the city were expelled and the son of Tarquinius Superbus had to flee from Rome to save his life. All the goods of the royal family were confiscated and the monarchy was formally abolished. The king, however, was not informed of these events and still had command of the Roman army that was besieging Ardea.

Nice example of a bronze 'bell' cuirass, of the model employed in Italy before the introduction of the 'muscle' cuirass. (*Photo and copyright by Athenea Prómakhos*)

If the army had remained loyal to him, it would have been easy for Tarquinius to march on Rome and reconquer the city. Before the king could organize himself, however, the leaders of the revolt sent an envoy to the Roman camp in Ardea informing the soldiers that the revolt had as its main objective removing the tyrant from the Roman throne. All the soldiers sided with the new provisional government, and Tarquinius Superbus was forced to go into exile together with his family. The ex-monarch went to the Etruscan city of Caere, where he started to reorganize himself for a future attack against Rome. The Etruscans, who considered Tarquinius the legitimate king of Rome, were ready to help him with funds and troops: after all, they could not accept the birth of a 'subversive' republican government in Rome and were extremely worried about the possibility that the Romans could emerge from their sphere of influence after having been ruled by three Etruscan kings. In 509 BC, Tarquinius Superbus marched against Rome at the head of a large military force, provided for him by the cities of Tarquinia and Veii. The Romans, led by their two new consuls (who had replaced the king as supreme commanders of the army), came out from the city and fought in the open field against Tarquinius. In what became known as the Battle of Silva Arsia, both sides suffered heavy casualties and the outcome of the clash was decided only after the centre of the Etruscan line collapsed. With this crushing defeat, at least for the moment, Tarquinia and Veii decided to stop their military operations against Rome. The exiled Tarquinius, however, did not give up and started to search for new and more powerful allies. After some difficult negotiations, Tarquinius was finally able to form a new anti-Roman alliance that comprised the Etruscans and the Latins; in particular, he obtained the support of Porsenna (king of Clusium), who was the most powerful of the Etruscan kings at the time. Clusium was rapidly emerging as the leading power of the Etruscan world, and therefore needed a brilliant victory in order to show its supremacy to all the other urban centres. At the head of a large army, Tarquinius and Porsenna obtained some astonishing victories over the Romans and besieged the city of Rome.

The young republic, however, was able to resist, thanks to the massive walls that had been built by Servius Tullius and to the courage of some young military leaders. Among these we should mention Horatius Cocles and Gaius Mucius. The former became a hero during the early phases of the Etruscan siege, when he alone was able to defend the Pons Sublicius (a bridge crossing the Tiber) against the assault of dozens of enemies who wanted to cross it. Horatius Cocles' heroic defence of the Pons Sublicius enabled his companions to destroy the bridge and thus save Rome. After the failure of this first assault, Porsenna decided to blockade the Tiber and besiege Rome. He believed that the defenders were already running out of food and that the city would be obliged to choose between starvation and surrender. While the Roman army was trapped inside the city walls, the Etruscans and their allies launched several raids in the

Composite hoplite cuirass made of linen and bronze scales. Hoplite armour was employed not only by the Romans and the Etruscans, but also by the Latins, who adopted the Greek panoply shortly after the Servian Reforms. (*Photo and copyright by Athenea Prómakhos*)

nearby countryside that caused serious damage to the Romans. Very soon, as expected by Porsenna, the situation became desperate for the republic: food was very scarce, the besieged city was crowded by thousands of peasants who had come from the countryside with their families and there was no hope of breaking the enemy positions. As a result, the Senate decided to send one of the youngest and most valorous military leaders to the Etruscan camp to kill Porsenna. The Romans hoped that the assassination of the enemy leader would leave the besieging army in a state of confusion. Gaius Mucius, against all odds, penetrated into the Etruscan camp without being seen and even entered into the tent of the enemy king: here, however, he found two men and was able to kill only one of them. Unluckily for him, the man he killed was a simple secretary, while the one who survived was Porsenna. After being captured by the Etruscans, Gaius Mucius decided to show his personal valour by 'punishing' his right hand that had killed the wrong man: the young Roman warrior put his right hand into one of the Etruscan camp fires and thus lost its use forever. Porsenna, impressed by this act of courage, decided to free Mucius, who became known as 'Scevola' (the 'left-handed') because he could now use only his left hand. After this episode, understanding that the Romans would have resisted for a long time despite their terrible difficulties, Porsenna finally decided that there was no point in supporting Tarquinius' attempts to regain power in Rome. A peace treaty was proposed to the besieged city, which was quite positive for the Etruscans; the Senate was forced to accept this, since the food stores of the city were practically empty.

Before his death in 495 BC, however, Tarquinius Superbus made a last attempt to reconquer Rome with the aid of the Latins during 499 BC. After having established his new base in the city of Tusculum, Tarquinius assembled an army of 40,000 Latins and fought the Roman consuls at the Battle of Lake Regillus. Some thirty Latin cities sent their troops to aid Tarquinius in what was the most important clash ever fought between the Romans and the Latins. The latter were by now organized into a political confederation known as the Latin League, the creation of which had been strongly sponsored by the Romans, who had been at the head of the confederation for several decades. With the birth of the Roman Republic, however, the Latins saw an opportunity to transform the League into an anti-Roman alliance with the objective of cancelling Rome's hegemony over their communities. The Battle of Lake Regillus was extremely violent, partly due to the participation of Roman exiles who fought on Tarquinius' side with the hope of restoring the monarchy in their home city. The old tyrant was wounded during the clash, which was finally decided by a desperate assault launched by the Roman cavalry. The Battle of Lake Regillus had some extremely important consequences for the history of Rome. Not only was it the last attempt by Tarquinius Superbus to reconquer his city, since the old tyrant died shortly afterwards, but it also

Phrygian helmet and leather 'muscle' cuirass, of the kind employed by Roman cavalrymen around the beginning of the First Punic War. (*Photo and copyright by Hetairoi*)

led to a definitive treaty known as the *Foedus Cassianum* in 493 BC, according to which all the cities of the Latin League recognized Rome as their supreme guide.

As we have seen, the period from 508–493 BC was a very difficult one for the Romans from a military point of view, but thanks to the many victories obtained during these years, Rome was able to free itself once and for all from Etruscan influence and to achieve complete dominance over the Latins. The army forged by Servius Tullius had been tested to the limit, but had been able to show all its positive features to great effect. During the following years, the young Roman Republic would fight more wars against the Etruscans and a series of bloody conflicts against the Volsci and Equi.

Chapter 3

The Birth of the Republic and the Wars Against the Oscans

The adoption of the new republican form of government, with two consuls at the head of the state and of the army, led to some significant changes in the organization of the Roman Army. The previous distinction between legions of *seniores* and *iuniores* was ended, with the *seniores* being abolished. The remaining legion was divided into two smaller legions, all of *iuniores* units, in order to have a single legion under the command of each consul. This way there was no possibility for a single man to assume complete control over all the military forces of the state, as had been possible during the period of the kings and in particular the reign of Tarquinius Superbus. The two new legions were much smaller and more flexible than the previous ones, each of them having a total of forty-five *centuriae*: twenty of the First Class, five of the Second Class, five of the Third Class, five of the Fourth Class, eight of the Fifth Class and one each of military engineers and military musicians. The organization of the cavalry, however, remained unchanged.

During most of the fifth century BC, especially after the *Foedus Cassianum* with the Latins, the Romans were involved in a series of wars against the Volsci and the Equi.

Bronze greaves, an important component of the Romano-Etruscan hoplite's panoply. (*Photo and copyright by Athenea Prómakhos*)

The Etruscans no longer posed a threat to the Roman and Latin lands located south of the Tiber. In 507 BC, after having abandoned the siege of Rome, Porsenna had tried to conquer some Latin lands by sending part of his military forces against the city of Ariccia. This city was besieged by the Etruscans for several months, but was able to resist as Rome had done before, and meanwhile the other cities of the Latin League and the Greeks from the colony of Cuma started to assemble an army to face Porsenna's forces in battle. The allied army defeated the Etruscans and saved Ariccia in 506 BC, thus bringing to an end all the expansionist plans of Porsenna. After the double failure of Rome and Ariccia, the Etruscans made no further attempts to occupy Rome or other cities of the Latium Vetus. Their most advanced outpost in the south remained Veii, which was strongly reinforced by the other Etruscan cities in order to stop the expansionist movement of the Romans directed towards the northern bank of the Tiber. For the moment, however, the Roman Army had enough to do in order to contain the raids of the Volsci and Equi. In 495 BC, shortly after the Battle of Lake Regillus, the Volsci invaded Rome's territory with the hope of surprising the Romans before they could recover from their losses suffered during the recent war with the Latins. Roman forces, however, were able to prevail and even destroyed the capital of the Volsci in retaliation. In 494 BC, the Romans launched a massive pre-emptive strike against all the Oscan peoples living in the mountainous areas that surrounded their territory. Rome's military forces were divided into three large contingents, each of which was sent against a different enemy: the Volsci, the Equi and the Sabines. Although the

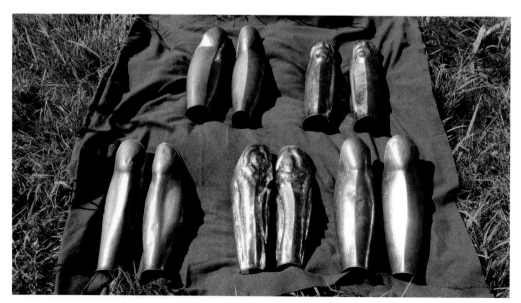

Various models of bronze greaves, employed by the Italic hoplites of the fifth and sixth century BC. (*Photo and copyright by Athenea Prómakhos*)

Romans achieved some crushing victories, their forces were too dispersed to obtain a decisive success over any of the three Oscan peoples.

After these early victories over the Volsci and the Equi, however, the Romans experienced a series of internal difficulties, mostly caused by the transition from monarchy to republic. With the adoption of the new form of government, very little had actually changed for the lower social classes of the city: the patricians, who controlled the Senate, determined the destiny of the state and the plebs could do nothing but obey the laws introduced by the aristocrats. Many of the *proletarii* had supported the process that led to the birth of the republic with the hope of obtaining more liberties and better conditions of life. After a few years, however, they understood that all their previous ambitions had come to naught. As a result, in 493 BC, the historical event known as the *secessio plebis* (secession of the plebs) took place. All the citizens of Rome, except for the rich patricians, abandoned the city and went to the Mons Aventinum (one of the Seven Hills), on which they built a temporary camp. By this the poor citizens were attempting to create their own independent settlement in order to become free from the negative influence of the nobles and of the new republican laws. The reasons behind the secession of the plebs were many, but foremost among them was the fact that the poor citizens could not express their political will by choosing their own representatives. The social and military reforms of Servius Tullius had been retained without modifications after the creation of the republic. The frequent military mobilizations for wars against the Oscan peoples also created discontent among the *plebei*, since these seriously curtailed the working activities of the poor citizens, who were all peasants. Producing grain in the fields was impossible if during most of the summer months the citizens were forced to march and fight at the orders of the patricians. The nobles exerted their dominance over the poor of Rome in many ways: there was a law, for example, which enabled them to arrest any *proletarius* who had some debts and was not able to pay them within a short period. In the most extreme cases, a poor citizen could also be enslaved by a patrician if he did not pay his debts.

During late 494 BC, the plebs had pressed the Senate to start a public discussion over all the important issues affecting them. However, while this was taking place the consuls were informed that the Volsci were marching on Rome. The leaders of the plebs, upon hearing this news, decided to oppose the ensuing mobilization, saying they would not fight against the enemies of Rome until all their social requests had been discussed by the Senate. Being in a desperate situation, since they could deploy only the cavalry and the hoplites if the plebs refused to mobilize, the aristocrats had to come to terms with the *proletarii*. It was formally promised that the laws regarding debts would be abolished soon after the end of the current military campaign and that

Romano-Etruscan infantryman of the Third Class, equipped with Montefortino helmet and oval shield. (*Photo and copyright by Antichi Popoli*)

all requests by the plebs would receive proper attention. The poor citizens, convinced by the promises of the Senate, thus marched against the Volsci during early 493 BC.

The campaign against the Volsci ended with victory for the Romans, who defeated their enemy on several occasions and found a capable military leader in Gneus Marcius, a rich aristocrat from one of the city's most prominent families who was one of the most reactionary patricians but had an incredible military talent. During the campaign of 493 BC, at the head of just a handful of men, he was able to capture a strong fortified settlement of the Volsci located at Corioli. Due to this unexpected success, Gneus Marcius received the nickname Coriolanus and became one of the new Roman heroes. When the victorious army returned to Rome, however, the Senate did not put into practice any of the promises that had been made to the plebs, and the *status quo* continued. At this point, as stated above, the poor citizens and most of the army launched a revolt against the aristocracy. They left Rome with their families and their few goods, going to the Mons Aventinum. This area had not yet been absorbed into the city and thus was outside the Servian Walls. In one of the most dramatic moments of the history of Rome to this point, the plebeians built a fortified camp on the hill and garrisoned it with most of the army. To solve this dangerous situation, which could have been lethal for Rome if any of its enemies had attacked, the Senate sent one of its members to the Aventinum in order to come to terms with the secessionists. The chosen senator was the well-known Menenius Agrippa, a man who was admired by the plebs for his brilliant public speeches. After some initial difficulties, Agrippa was able to convince the plebs to abandon Mons Aventinum and return to Rome. He explained to the rebellious citizens that they were as important as the patricians for the existence of the Roman Republic, and that the new state would never survive if its social classes were fighting against each other. In addition, and more importantly, Agrippa made some concessions to the plebs on behalf of the Senate: for the first time in Rome's history, it was agreed that the *proletarii* could choose two political representatives. These were known as the *tribuni plebis*, who were allowed to participate in all the discussions of the Senate in order to defend the interests of the poor citizens.

While the events of 493 BC ended in a positive fashion for the Roman state, the agreement that had been reached between the patricians and the plebs was not yet a definitive one. Tensions continued during the following years, culminating in 491 BC when Coriolanus was exiled from Rome. The war hero had never fully recognized the right of the plebs to have two *tribuni*, and thus continued to act as if nothing had changed. Due to his behaviour, Coriolanus was sued by the tribunes of the plebs and was accused of having stolen the spoils of war captured during the most recent campaign against the Volsci. Refusing to be judged, Coriolanus left Rome and went into exile to the territory of the Volsci in search of revenge. He was soon able to obtain

Romano-Etruscan archer of the Fourth Class, using his wooden longbow. (*Photo and copyright by Antichi Popoli*)

the full support of his former enemies and was given command of their army, at the head of which he initiated a new war with the objective of destroying Rome forever.

The ex-Roman general developed a very intelligent war plan. He sent half of his forces against the lands of the Latins, in order to prevent them from sending any reinforcements to the Roman Republic, while the other half of the Volsci, under his personal command, ravaged the countryside of Rome to destroy all the reserves of grain. With the Roman Army essentially trapped inside the Servian Walls, the Volsci could do anything they wanted in the surrounding fields. Coriolanus had given precise orders: all the properties and reserves of the plebs had to be destroyed, while those of the patricians were preserved. By so doing he hoped to cause the outbreak of renewed civil strife between the plebs and the patricians inside the besieged city. Coriolanus hoped that the nobles, feeling menaced by the poorer citizens, would have opened the gates of the city to the Volsci and probably would have welcomed him as their new king. During the following months, however, Rome was able to resist as the Volsci did not have enough warriors to permanently besiege the city.

Coriolanus continued to fight and win in the countryside, attacking and defeating several Latin cities, but the war entered a period of stalemate. The Volsci tried to enlarge the anti-Roman front by also involving the Equi in their campaign against Rome, but this was not enough to change the course of the conflict. Eventually, understanding that there was no possibility of the Volsci opening a breach in the Servian Walls, Coriolanus decided to attend peace talks with Roman ambassadors. The Roman emissaries went to the Volsci camp together with Coriolanus' relatives, who had remained in Rome after the general's exile. After reconciling with his wife and sons, Coriolanus decided to suspend the hostilities between the Volsci and Rome. A temporary truce was accepted by both sides and the conflict came to an end. Rome had again been on the verge of destruction, but once more the tenacious defence of the citizens and soldiers had been able to save the Republic. After these events, the great military leader known as Coriolanus disappeared from history, but hostilities between the Oscan peoples and Rome continued with even greater intensity during the following decades.

In 484 BC, the Romans attacked both the Volsci and the Equi, with the aim of conquering the main settlements of the Oscan peoples. Although they achieved several victories against the Equi, they suffered a crushing defeat at the hands of the Volsci after a major pitched battle. The Roman Republic turned against the Sabines in 475 BC, together with the Latins who by now had the same political interests as Rome. While the Sabines were defeated, the Romans and their allies were prevented from obtaining a complete victory due to a new attack launched by the Volsci that menaced Rome. The Roman Army faced a large combined force of Volsci and Equi in battle in 471 BC, but at a crucial moment a large number of Roman soldiers deserted and the battle

Oscan warrior with 'pot' helmet, trilobate cuirass, round shield and bronze greaves. This kind of equipment was employed by several Italic peoples and was perfectly suited to the mountainous terrain of the Apennines. (*Photo and copyright by Confraternita del Leone / Historia Viva*)

thus proved indecisive. This episode of mass desertion was caused by the internal tensions that shattered the stability of the Roman Republic, the civil strife between the patricians and the plebeians having entered into a new phase of open conflict. The plebs considered the wars against the Oscan peoples as only having positive results for the aristocrats, and thus tried to hamper the efforts of the consuls during the course of the military operations. In 468 BC, the decisive pitched battle that the Romans had been seeking for years was fought on the territory of the Equi, and despite being in clear numerical inferiority the Romans and their Latin allies obtained a great success over the Oscan peoples after several days of harsh fighting. The capital of the Equi was occupied, and during the following year a peace treaty was signed between the Roman Republic and the Equi. In 463 BC, Rome was devastated by the plague, which caused great losses to the population. The Oscans took advantage of this event to ravage the Roman countryside and obtain some minor victories, but during the following year they were defeated again.

In 459 BC, the Oscan peoples attacked Tusculum, one of the Latin cities that had supported Rome during the recent wars. The Romans sent their army against the Equi who were besieging Tusculum and saved the city from destruction. At the same time, they also sent troops against the Volsci and obtained another victory. This new conflict ended with a massacre of Equi warriors, perpetrated by the Romans as a punishment for the attack against Tusculum. The Romans found themselves at war again with the Equi and Sabines in 458 BC. As a result, they had to divide their military forces to face two enemies at the same time and started to suffer some serious difficulties. One of the two Roman armies was surrounded by the Equi in mountainous terrain, while the other was unable to engage with the enemy. In order to deal with this unexpected situation, the Senate decided to nominate a dictator who would assume the direction of the military operations. In case of military emergencies, the Roman constitution prescribed the possibility of choosing an experienced commander and giving him the absolute powers of dictatorship for a short period of time. On some occasions it had proved difficult to maintain a coherent strategic line when the leadership of Rome's military forces was in the hands of two consuls with contrasting personal ambitions. The Senate chose as dictator Cincinnatus, a man who had great capabilities and who was loved by the plebeians because of his personal charisma. Cincinnatus was able to raise a third army in just a few hours by recruiting all the able-bodied citizens who had remained in Rome, and marched outside the walls to save the Roman troops that were under enemy siege north of the city. During a terrible night battle, Cincinnatus attacked the Equi from the rear and caused them serious losses. During the clash the besieged Romans also attacked the enemy, and thus the defeat of the Equi became a rout. After this success Cincinnatus marched against the Volsci and defeated them.

Oscan warrior with 'pot' helmet, trilobate cuirass, oval shield and bronze greaves. This veteran fighter could come from any of the warlike peoples living in central Italy: Sabines, Equi, Volsci or Marsi. (*Photo and copyright by Confraternita del Leone / Historia Viva*)

Oscan warrior with 'pot' helmet, trilobate cuirass, oval shield and bronze greaves. The triangular cuirass, consisting of three discs, was the most distinctive element of the Oscan panoply. (*Photo and copyright by Confraternita del Leone / Historia Viva*)

Thanks to the unexpected ascendancy of a new military commander, Rome had been able to obtain decisive victories over the Oscan peoples and could now look forward to several years of peace. During this short respite, however, the internal tensions between patricians and plebeians became a serious problem again. The poorest social classes started to demand from the Roman Senate the enacting of a written constitution: until that time, Rome had been governed by oral laws that were usually modified and applied by the patricians in whatever way was most convenient for them. In 451 BC, a special commission of ten men, known as the *decemviri*, was nominated to write down the fundamental laws of the Roman Republic. After completing their task, however, these men did not abandon their prominent positions and started to rule the city as a true oligarchy. It had been intended that after writing down the new constitution of Rome they would renounce their powers. When the *decemviri* started to rule as dictators themselves, the plebs revolted against them. The army, which was camped just outside Rome for a minor campaign against the Oscan peoples, marched on the city in order to restore democracy and remove the *decemviri*. As proved by these events, the Roman Republic was still young and had many internal problems. However, after the removal of the *decemviri* in 449 BC, Rome did not experience any other internal strife for many decades.

Finally, during 446 BC, the long and terrible clash with the Oscan peoples came to an end. The Volsci and the Equi, after having assembled all their military forces into a single army, marched against the Latin territories and ravaged many of them. At this point they moved against Rome, with the intention of destroying their mortal enemy forever. The Romans, who had remained quite passive during the early phase of the campaign, were forced to deploy their whole army and fight a decisive battle at Corbione. This clash, the largest ever fought between the Romans and the Oscans, ended with a complete Roman victory. The Volsci and the Equi, after suffering terrible losses, were forced to return to their native territories. Although during the following decades they fought several other minor wars against the Roman Republic, they were always defeated by the Romans in short order and without causing any major difficulties. Thanks to the victory at the Battle of Corbione, Rome could finally assume a prominent position over the whole territory of the Latium Vetus and start planning expansionist moves directed against the Etruscans on the northern bank of the Tiber.

The first target of the Romans was Veii, which had been a deadly enemy of Rome since the early days of the monarchy. As we have seen, the Etruscans of Veii strongly opposed the adoption of a republican form of government in Rome and supported with all their forces the attempts at reconquest by Tarquinius Superbus. In 482 BC, Rome resumed hostilities against Veii, but on a small scale and with low intensity: during the following years, the priority of the Roman Republic was defeating the

Umbrian warrior. Some elements of his equipment, like the trilobate cuirass and bronze greaves, are clearly Oscan, while others (like the Montefortino helmet or ceremonial spear) are the result of the strong military influence exerted by the Gauls over the Umbrians. (*Photo and copyright by Confraternita del Leone / Historia Viva*)

Oscan peoples. As a result, the Romans did not launch any invasion of the territory surrounding Veii, and the Etruscans of the city were similarly watchful. Curiously, one of the most important aristocratic families of Rome, the Gens Fabia, was charged with conducting this small-scale war against Veii on behalf of the entire Roman population. In practice, the war with Veii became a private affair for the Fabii, who had a lot to gain from this state of continuous hostility existing between their city and the nearby Etruscans. During the following decades, while the Fabii conducted small raids and incursions in the countryside of Veii to destroy or steal the food reserves of the enemy, the main Roman forces concentrated upon fighting against the Oscans.

In 438 BC, a few years after Rome defeated the Volsci and the Equi, a new state of full-scale war commenced between the Roman Republic and Veii; the city had helped the Oscans (in particular the Sabines) on many occasions, and the Romans could not forget this. The city of Fidenae, with the support of Veii, rebelled against Rome, but the consuls soon marched against the Etruscans and defeated them. The king of Veii was killed during this clash, but the Romans were not able to occupy Fidenae. In 435 BC, while Rome was shattered by the plague, the soldiers of Veii and Fidenae tried to occupy it, but their offensive was badly planned and ended with a massive Roman counterattack that caused the fall of Fidenae. Sometime after these events, the Etruscans of Veii again attacked Rome, but were once more defeated and the city of Fidenae was reoccupied by the Romans. Rome, in order to finally end the series of clashes with its mortal enemies, decided to raze Fidenae to the ground and enslave all the inhabitants of the city in order to prevent any further alliance with Veii. After some years of relative peace, the Romans started to besiege the Etruscan city for several months every year in an attempt to destroy the economy of their rival, but without damaging their own agricultural activities (when the Roman soldiers had to work in their fields, the siege was temporarily abandoned). This Roman strategy, however, did not work well and Veii continued to resist without major problems. It became clear that a proper 'full-time' siege was needed if Rome wanted to finally defeat the Etruscan city. As a result, in 406 BC, the Senate finally decided to start paying the soldiers in order to employ them for the whole year in the siege of Veii: this was an extremely important innovation for the Roman Army, marking a first step towards professionalism. The soldiers, thanks to the introduction of regular pay (*stipendium*), could serve through all the seasons of the year and no longer needed to return home in order to work as peasants in their fields. As the siege of Veii became permanent the Roman war effort likewise stepped up and the Senate thus had to find the economic resources needed to pay so many soldiers for a long period, which proved a difficult undertaking. The siege of Veii continued for another ten years, with the Etruscan city supported by the Falisci and the Capenati, two peoples who lived in northern Latium and had long been under

Warrior of the Picentes. The 'pot' helmet and javelin are clearly Oscan, while the chainmail and trousers have clearly been imported from the Celtic territories of northern Italy. (*Photo and copyright by Confraternita del Leone / Historia Viva*)

Etruscan influence. On several occasions the besieging Romans were attacked from the rear by the Falisci and the Capenati, but were always able to resist and maintain their positions without breaking the siege. When it became clear that Veii was on the verge of being conquered by the Romans, the political leaders of the besieged city sent formal requests for help to all the other major Etruscan centres. The Etruscans, however, were facing a new Celtic menace from northern Italy and thus were in no condition to send part of their armies to the rescue of Veii. In order to obtain a final victory over the Etruscans, the Romans decided to nominate a dictator; their choice was Marcus Furius Camillus, the best military leader available to them at the time. Camillus inflicted a crushing defeat on the Falisci and Capenati and then concentrated all his efforts against Veii, which finally fell during 396 BC.

Chapter 4

The Sack of Rome and the Conquest of Etruria

Following the fall of Veii, the Roman Republic seemed to be ready to launch a massive offensive against the Etruscan cities of northern Latium; however, they were prevented from doing so by unpredictable events. A new and mysterious force originating from the heart of Continental Europe – the Celts of Brennus, called Gauls by the Romans – started to move from northern Italy into central Italy. The first mass migration of Celts towards the plains of northern Italy took place around 600 BC, when the great warlord Bellovesus led a coalition of tribes across the Alps. The most important Celtic group marching towards Italy was represented by the Senones, who were accompanied by several other minor tribes: the Aeduii, Ambarri, Arverni, Aulerci and Carnutes. Initially the advance of the Senones encountered very little resistance and the newcomers were able to found several important settlements. During the following decades, the Celts settled in Lombardy continued the expansionist process initiated by Bellovesus and decided to move further south. They soon reached the Po River, around which some of the most fertile Italian plains were located. This region, however, was already inhabited by the Etruscans, who had built several important cities there, and the Celts were obliged to fight in order to continue their advance. The Senones were gradually joined by other important tribes, like those of the Insubres, who founded an important new centre at Mediolanum (present-day Milan) from where to continue their advance.

The Senones remained the main driving force of Celtic expansionism in Italy; according to Roman writers, they were the most violent and ferocious of all Gauls. What we know for sure is that they continued to move south, defeating the Etruscans and the other Italic peoples they found on their way. Before the Celtic invasions, the Etruscans were the most powerful people of Italy, their great cities dominating most of the peninsula and enjoying complete control over all trade routes. The arrival of the Celts changed all this, since the Etruscans had to abandon their expansionist ambitions in order to defend their home territories from Celtic incursions. The Etruscans fought more or less like the contemporary Greeks, with phalanxes of hoplites made up of heavy infantrymen, but their military formations had never faced an enemy as wild as the Gauls. By 400 BC, all the Etruscan cities of the Po Valley had fallen to the Celts, who had been able to advance further south. The northern areas of central Italy on the Adriatic coast were thus occupied by the Senones, who defeated the local Picentes tribe.

Map of ancient northern Italy, showing the areas inhabited by the three main peoples of the region: Ligures, Celts/Gauls and Veneti. The Raeti and Camunni, who were minor populations living in the Alps, were gradually absorbed by the expanding Celts. (*CC BY-SA 3.0, Wikimedia User Nancy Todd*)

In 390 BC the Senones, guided by their great military leader Brennus, decided that the moment had come to move further south, with the objective of conquering the great Etruscan cities of Tuscany as well as Rome. The first target of the new Celtic advance was the Etruscan centre of Clusum, at the time an ally of Rome. The Romans sent an embassy to Brennus, warning that an attack against Clusum would be interpreted as a declaration of war against the Republic. During negotiations, however, a skirmish broke out between the Etruscan/Roman ambassadors and the Celtic representatives. During the clash one of the Senones was killed, and thereafter the Gauls decided to besiege Clusum. Since the Gallic warlord had been killed by one of the three Roman ambassadors, Brennus sent a delegation to Rome demanding the handing over of the Roman representatives in order to obtain justice. Clearly, events in Clusum had given the Celtic leader a perfect *casus belli*. The Romans responded to Brennus' requests by electing the three ambassadors as military tribunes with consular power. As a result, the Celts abandoned their siege of Clusum and marched south against Rome with revenge on their mind. The Romans knew practically nothing of the Celts and their

Gaul warrior with Agen-Port helmet and chainmail. (*Photo and copyright by Les Ambiani*)

battle tactics, having never fought a battle against them. The Roman Republic was able to assemble a large army totalling 35,000 men to face Brennus, who commanded more or less 40,000 warriors. It is important to note, however, that only 11,000 of the Romans were well-trained soldiers. These elite troops were organized into two legions, while the remaining 24,000 men were a hasty levy of untrained *proletarii*. A decisive clash was fought on the Allia River, just a few miles north of Rome.

According to ancient sources, the Gauls of Brennus advanced much more rapidly than the Romans expected, Rome's leaders having probably planned to fight the decisive battle on Etruscan territory rather than so close to home. While the Romans were still mobilizing their troops, Brennus was able to cover a large distance in just a few days. Having been surprised by the enemy, the Romans had no time to build a fortified camp as they usually did, and were even not able to pay respect to their gods before the battle (something considered unacceptable to the traditional religious view of the Romans). Being outnumbered by their enemies and knowing practically nothing of their tactics, the Romans decided to deploy all their forces in a single and very long line: this was in order to avoid any possible outflanking manoeuvre by the enemy, but such a disposition made the Roman centre extremely thin. A number of Roman soldiers, possibly the badly trained *proletarii* who had been hastily called to serve, were put in reserve and placed on a hill located to the rear of the Roman right wing. The Gauls launched a general and furious attack with all their forces along the whole line of battle, and after a brief clash – during which the Roman soldiers could not manoeuvre due to their static formations – the Celts were able to break the line at various points. The legionaries on the Roman left abandoned their positions and fled to the nearby city of Veii, which had been recently conquered by the Romans, while the Roman centre was completely annihilated by the enemy charge. On the right, the Republican forces were able to maintain their positions a little longer thanks to the presence of the reserves and of the hill, but finally these soldiers were also obliged to fall back and retreated to Rome. Analyzing the little information we have of the battle, it is clear that the Romans panicked as soon as the Celts launched their assault: these fierce warriors from the north with their strange weapons and clothes, screaming like eagles and playing mysterious musical instruments, looked terrible in the eyes of the Romans. Brennus and his warlords were surprised at how easy their victory had been. Many thousands of Romans had been killed during the rout that followed the breaking of the Roman line, while Celtic losses were minimal. Rome no longer had a proper army and seemed ready to be conquered by the Gauls.

After despoiling their dead enemies, the warriors of Brennus marched towards the gates of Rome, where they were greatly surprised to find the city almost defenceless. The gates were open and there were no soldiers guarding the walls, the Romans having decided to defend only a portion of their city. Since there were not enough soldiers to guard all the Servian Walls, all the able-bodied men and political leaders had retreated to the Capitoline Hill. This strongly fortified citadel inside Rome was located on higher ground which could be easily defended by a small force of men. All the weapons and provisions available in the city were massed on the Capitoline Hill, where the ruling families of Rome (those of the senators) had also found refuge. Most of the common people abandoned the city and went to nearby centres that were allies of Rome. The Flamen of Quirinus (the most important sacred symbol of Rome) and the Vestal Virgins who maintained it were also transferred to a nearby city. Some of the elder men, mostly patricians and senators, decided instead to remain in the city and await the arrival of the enemy. Brennus led his men into Rome and started to plunder all the houses. When the Celts reached the Forum, they found many elderly patricians and senators waiting for them. The proud Roman aristocrats were immobile, to the point that the Gauls could not understand if they were real men or sculptures, but once the Celts realized they were the aristocrats of Rome they killed them all. The plundering of the city was terrible: all the houses were destroyed by fire and many streets were piled high with bodies. Apparently, the Celts decided to devastate the lower city to break the morale of the defenders garrisoning the Capitoline Hill. However, despite hearing the roaring of the flames and the screaming of the victims, the soldiers guarding the citadel did not abandon their positions. After several days of sacking and killing, the Gauls understood that the defenders of Capitoline Hill had enough provisions to resist a long siege. As a result, Brennus decided to launch an attack against the citadel.

The Celts, unlike the Romans, were not experts in siege warfare. They were unable to build siege machines, and usually conquered enemy cities only after the defenders had run out of provisions. In this case, however, Brennus could not wait for such a long time: the allies of Rome were already assembling new military forces to confront the invaders and thus the Celts could have been trapped inside Rome while besieging the Capitoline Hill. The first assault of the Gauls was a costly failure: once the Celts were halfway up the hill, the defenders launched a deadly counter-attack that caused terrible losses to Brennus' warriors. After such a defeat, the Celtic warlord understood that it was impossible to conquer the Capitoline Hill with frontal attacks. While these events took place inside the city, Brennus sent reconnaissance parties into the countryside surrounding Rome with orders to capture any supplies that they could find, as the devastated city could not feed the invaders for long.

During these raiding operations the Celts were beaten by the allies of Rome, led by Marcus Furius Camillus. Camillus, who had conquered Veii and was the most capable Roman general of his time, was no longer in the service of Rome. In 391 BC, like Coriolanus before him, he had been forced to leave his home city in exile for

Gaul warrior with Agen–Port helmet and leather armour. (*Photo and copyright by Contoutos Atrebates*)

Celtic warrior from *Gallia Cisalpina*. (*Photo and copyright by Contoutos Atrebates*)

political reasons. Thanks to his great military victories, he had started to be considered as a menace to democracy by many of his rivals, who feared his great popularity with the people. False accusations were created to put Camillus in a bad light, and thus the general had no choice but to leave Rome and move to the allied Latin city of Ardea. When the Celts occupied Rome, the exiled general decided to put aside the treatment he had received and to help his former city in any possible way. He recruited an army of Roman allies, comprising a large number of Latin warriors and Roman survivors who had fled to Veii. Using guerrilla methods and knowing well the terrain over which the Celtic raiding parties were moving, Camillus caused serious losses to the Gauls.

After hearing of the defeats suffered by his raiding forces, Brennus decided to launch a final attack against the enemy citadel: this time, however, the Celts would try to reach the top of the Capitoline Hill by climbing it at night. The special operation was to be conducted by a small number of chosen warriors, all expert climbers. The Gauls were able to reach the top of the hill, but were said to have been discovered by the sacred geese of Juno, which made such a noise that they alerted the Roman defenders, who repulsed them. The famous episode of the Capitoline geese is obviously an invention, but thanks to the ancient sources describing it we can plausibly suppose that the Gauls did indeed organize a night attack that was repulsed by the Romans.

During the following days, without any hope of conquering the enemy positions, the Gauls started to suffer from famine and pestilence. Brennus was still determined to conquer the citadel, but his warlords were by now impatient to return home. As a result, the great leader was obliged to start negotiations with the Romans, the two sides agreeing on a ransom of a thousand pounds of gold. When the Romans delivered the gold, the Celts tried to cheat about its weight. According to tradition, when the Romans protested that they had brought the required amount, Brennus tossed his heavy sword on the scale and made the famous expression '*Vae victis!*' ('Woe to the defeated!'). After finally being paid much more than the Romans had agreed, the Gauls abandoned the devastated city and went back to their territories in northern Italy. Apparently, Brennus had realized that conquering Rome was impossible, and thus what had started as an invasion transformed itself into a raiding operation. The Romans, however, had been humiliated and had lost most of their wealth; they never forgot this great defeat of their early history, considering the Gauls as the most serious menace to their security.

The Sack of Rome initiated a new phase in relations between Celts and Romans, which would be marked by the implacable hatred of the latter for the heirs of Brennus. Despite the scale of their military disaster, Rome would need just a few decades to fully recover: the city was rebuilt, new political and military leaders emerged, the military defences were improved and the expansionist ambitions towards southern Etruria

Some products of the Celtic blacksmiths. (*Photo and copyright by Les Trimatrici*)

were restored. The Celtic invasion of central Italy proved only a temporary setback, with no enduring consequences for Rome. It made clear, however, that the Gauls were a new and important military power in the peninsula, with whom the Romans would have to fight again in the near future.

After the terrible events of 390 BC, the political life of Rome continued to be dominated by Camillus, who could count on the decisive support of the army. The brilliant general had to face a series of military threats as the traditional enemies of Rome viewed the temporary difficulties of the city as an opportunity to regain the territories that they had recently lost. In 389 BC, several Etruscan cities arranged an alliance with what remained of the Volsci and the Equi to invade Roman territory. Camillus had no choice but to use all the remaining resources of the city and divided the Roman Army into three parts. The first was sent to Veii in order to protect it from Etruscan attacks from the north; the second was deployed in the countryside surrounding Rome to protect the city from enemy incursions; the third, commanded by Camillus himself, moved against the Oscans. The great Roman general was rapidly

Arrow-heads and spear-heads produced by the Celtic blacksmiths. (*Photo and copyright by Les Trimatrici*)

able to defeat both the Volsci and the Equi before they could join forces with the Etruscans. After securing Roman control over Latium Vetus, Camillus moved north and also repulsed the Etruscan attack. In a single year the strategic situation of central Italy had been restored to the *status quo*: now the Roman Republic could start planning the progressive occupation of Etruscan territories.

The Etruscans had been seriously damaged by the Celtic invasion of central Italy. Many of their most important urban centres had been sacked by the invaders and they had been forced to abandon all their flourishing settlements in the Po Valley. In 388 BC, the Romans invaded the territory of Tarquinia and occupied two minor Etruscan settlements without difficulties. During 386 BC, in retaliation, the Etruscans besieged and occupied the city of Sutrium, an ally of Rome. Camillus then marched against the Etruscans and defeated them, reconquering Sutrium. After these military events, Rome suspended its operations against the Etruscans for several years while it consolidated its prominence over Latium and repulsed some minor Celtic incursions directed towards central Italy. In 358 BC, the Etruscans of Tarquinia resumed hostilities against Rome in a bid to defend what remained of their influence in northern Latium. Initially the Romans suffered some defeats during this war, but in 356 BC the army of Tarquinia was crushed in a major pitched battle. At this point all the Etruscan cities understood that the only way to defeat Rome and oppose its expansionism was to join their forces into a large military alliance (something that they had done quite rarely during their history). In 357 BC, a large army comprising contingents from all the Etruscan cities marched south with the intention of conquering and pillaging the strategic area located at the mouth of the Tiber. The Romans found themselves in great difficulty due to the superior numbers of the enemy, but were eventually able to launch a massive offensive against the Etruscans. The Etruscans were taken by surprise, being attacked while pillaging the Roman stores along the course of the river. In the ensuing battle the Etruscans suffered heavy casualties and 8,000 of their soldiers were captured by the Romans. The attempted invasion had turned into a disaster and marked a turning of the tide, as after such a crushing defeat the Etruscans were no longer capable of mounting offensive operations against the Romans.

In 355 BC, the Romans marched on Tarquinia, aiming to defeat the most important of the Etruscan cities. After a fiercely fought battle the Etruscan city was conquered and

A warlord and his retainers from the territory of *Gallia Cisalpina*. (*Photo and copyright by Les Trimatrici*)

submitted. Most of the local aristocrats were executed in order to deprive Tarquinia of its political leaders. Two years later, the Romans turned their attention to the city of Caere and marched their military forces into the heart of Etruria. Having seen what had happened to Tarquinia when it resisted, the Etruscans of Caere preferred to surrender without a fight and became vassals of Rome. In 351 BC, all the remaining Etruscan cities mobilized their forces for a new war against Rome, but when the Roman Army entered Etruria they surrendered in order to avoid any further devastation. The options for the Etruscans were by now clear: pressed by the Gauls in the north and the Romans in the south, they had to choose which of their enemies to accept as overlords. The Roman Republic was the obvious choice, since the Romans had so much in common with the Etruscans. A final Etruscan rebellion was easily crushed by the Romans in 311–309 BC, and during the following decades the Romans were finally able to absorb the Etruscan world into their sphere of influence.

Chapter 5

The Samnite Wars and the
Reform of the Roman Army

While the Romans were heavily involved in the wars that transformed their city into the dominant military power of central Italy, the warlike people of the Samnites gradually became the most powerful community of southern Italy. The Samnites were part of the Oscan peoples and thus had much in common with the Volsci and the Equi. Unlike them, however, the Samnites were a confederation of tribes and thus could deploy armies with impressive numbers. After arriving in southern Italy during the Oscan migrations, the Samnites started to expand from their initial settlements. Within a few decades they were able to gain control over all the interior areas of the region, forcing the Greeks to live in their coastal cities. The original area settled by the Samnites was entirely covered by mountains and was located south of the Latium Vetus. The Samnites first came into contact with the Roman Republic after Rome's defeat of the Volsci and the Equi. While the Samnites were used to the harsh conditions of the Apennines, they did not practise much agriculture, being mostly shepherds. Although they did practise commerce with the other peoples of Italy, they generally preferred raiding and pillaging in order to augment their possessions. Their tribal society, based on villages, had much more personal freedom than in the city of Rome, where the patricians were still dominant. In addition, despite their lands having few natural resources, the Samnites were able to produce excellent weapons. The warriors of this fierce people were all equipped as light infantrymen, used to moving very rapidly in the broken terrain of their mountains and valleys. Unlike the Romans, they did not fight in close formations such as the phalanx, preferring to strike their enemies from a distance with their javelins.

As we have seen in the previous chapters, the Oscan peoples of Latium had been able to defeat the Romans only when they employed hit-and-run tactics on broken terrain; when fighting against the Roman phalanx on open ground they had been defeated on most occasions. Whereas the territory of Latium is mostly covered by plains, that where the Samnites lived was entirely covered by mountains. This meant that if there was war between the Romans and the Samnites, neither side would have been able to prevail without reforming its military forces: the Romans would have never been able to crush Samnite resistance in the harsh terrain of Samnium, while the

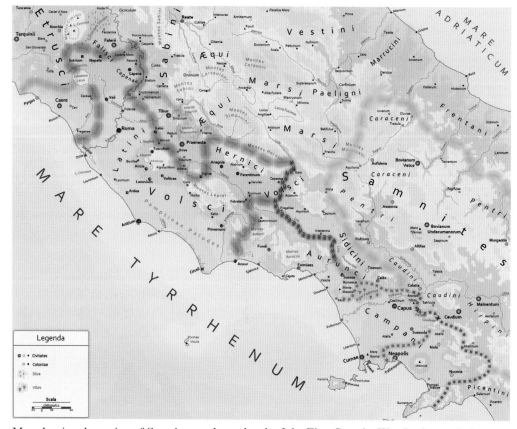

Map showing the region of Samnium at the outbreak of the First Samnite War. In the south, between the territories of the Romans and those of the Samnites, it is possible to see the area inhabited by the Campanians. (*CC BY-SA 3.0, Wikimedia User ColdEel and Ahenobarbus*)

Samnites would have been unable to defeat the Romans in a pitched battle fought on open ground. The Romans and Samnites concluded a treaty of alliance in 354 BC after coming into contact for the first time along the border of southern Latium. At that time both sides were heavily involved on other fronts and thus preferred to maintain positive relations with each other. The Romans, as we have seen, were completing their conquest of Etruria, while the Samnites were expanding towards the coastal areas of Campania.

Campania, situated south of Latium, was politically divided into two parts: in the west, along the coast, were the fertile plains dominated by the Greeks and the local peaceful population of the Campanians (whose main city was the rich agricultural centre of Capua); in the east, in the centre of the Italian peninsula, were the Apennine mountains where the warlike Samnite tribes lived. The Samnites had long wanted to conquer the rich lands of the Campanians in order to improve their agricultural

Samnite warrior with Chalcidian helmet. He is wearing some magnificent examples of a trilobate cuirass and a war belt (both made of bronze). These two pieces of equipment were used by the majority of the Oscan warriors. (*Photo and copyright by Confraternita del Leone / Historia Viva*)

production. The territory of coastal Campania was extremely fertile, to the point that this area was known as Campania Felix (fertile or happy countryside) during Antiquity. As a result, both the Romans and the Samnites had ambitions to conquer it. In 343 BC, knowing that their military forces were unable to stop Samnite aggression, the Campanians of Capua 'donated' their city to the Romans in exchange for military protection against the Samnite tribes. Despite the Romans being surprised by this political move, after some hesitation they decided to include Capua in their sphere of influence. This action brought to an end the alliance that had existing for more than ten years between Rome and the Samnites, opening the way for a Samnite attack against Capua.

The First Samnite War started in 343 BC. According to ancient sources, when the Capuans offered their city to Rome the Samnites were already besieging it and the situation of the defenders was becoming desperate. As a result, the Romans had no time to waste if they wished to save Capua from the Samnites. The Roman Army was divided into two parts: one was sent to Campania with orders to attack the besiegers of Capua, while the other marched into Samnium to raid Samnite lands in retaliation for the losses suffered by the Campanians. The troops moving against the Samnites at Capua fought a first battle against the enemy at Mons Gaurus, not far from the besieged city. The Romans were confident of an easy victory over the Samnites, but they knew very little of the battle tactics employed by their new enemies. In the opening phase of the clash the Romans launched a cavalry charge against the Samnite line, but the assault was a complete failure due to the broken terrain on which it was conducted. The Roman horsemen, forced to move very slowly, became an easy target for the deadly javelins of the Samnite warriors. The clash between the Roman and Samnite infantry lasted for several hours and ended with no clear winner. When darkness descended on the battlefield, although the Samnites abandoned their camp the Romans had not obtained a decisive success. However, the Romans had learned an important lesson: the Samnites were much more determined fighters than any other of the Italic peoples they had faced before.

Another pitched battle was fought on the Campanian front shortly after, at Suessula. This time the Romans were able to inflict heavier casualties on the Samnites, attacking while their enemies were dispersed in the nearby countryside in search of food and other provisions. The surprise attack of the Romans ended with the occupation of the opposing camp, the Samnites were routed and their forces fled. Without a base or food reserves, they had no choice but to suspend the siege of Capua. The Romans had demonstrated their superiority in fighting on flat terrain, while the Samnites had shown major deficiencies in relation to logistics. The Samnite forces had great difficulties in operating far from their homeland and had little experience of invasions

Samnite/Lucanian warrior with Chalcidian helmet and oval shield. The Lucanians were equipped exactly like their Samnite 'cousins'. (*Photo and copyright by Confraternita del Leone / Historia Viva*)

conducted with long supply lines. However, whereas the Romans had the upper hand in Campania, the military situation in Samnium was completely different: here the Romans marched across the high mountains without even seeing the enemy warriors, suffering heavy casualties due to the local climate and the Samnites' hit-and-run tactics. The Samnites were masters of skirmishes and ambushes, killing dozens of Romans before they could adopt a defensive formation. They refused to fight a pitched battle on their home territory and the Romans could not find their settlements, so this first Roman invasion of Samnium was a complete failure.

The Romans sent another army into Samnite territory in 341 BC, but this had more or less the same result as the previous attack. As a result, since the Samnites were in no condition to resume their offensive against Capua and the Romans were unable to conquer Samnium, the two warring sides decided to put an end to hostilities and sign a peace treaty. According to this, the *status quo* was restored: the Romans and the Samnites were again allies, the only difference being that the Samnites renounced their expansionist plans involving Capua, which now formally became a Roman subject. The Roman Republic had thus obtained a first stronghold in Campania, thanks to which it could start planning for the inclusion of all Campanian territory in its sphere of influence. Despite the good intentions expressed by the peace treaty, it was clear that both sides were already preparing for a new war. The Romans could not accept the existence of such a powerful rival just south of their borders, and the Samnites considered the failed siege of Capua as only a temporary setback and were still determined to gain complete control over the agricultural production and trade routes of Campania. During the campaigns fought on Samnite territory the Romans had started to understand that their army had some organizational problems, since it always needed to deploy the full phalanx in order to achieve positive results. This was not possible on the broken territory of the Apennine mountains, and thus constituted a serious limitation for the Roman military machine.

Before resuming hostilities against the mountain fighters of Samnium, however, the Roman Republic had to embark on another unexpected war in Latium Vetus. In 340 BC, the Romans invited all the cities of the Latin League to send their political representatives to Rome in order to discuss some important issues. These included the creation of a single state comprising both Rome and the Latin cities, which would be peacefully absorbed into the Roman Republic. Relations between Rome and the Latin League had been extremely positive for decades, so the Romans were sure that the Latins would accept their offer to form a single state. However, the Latins were strongly jealous of their national independence and refused to submit. They had no intention of becoming subjects of Rome. They would accept a political union only if their communities received a high degree of representation in Rome. The Latins, for

Samnite/Lucanian warrior armed with spear and throwing javelin. This is a perfect example of the standard light equipment used by most of the Oscan fighters. (*Photo and copyright by Confraternita del Leone/Historia Viva*)

example, required that one of the two consuls elected every year had to be a Latin in order to have a perfect balance of power between Romans and Latins. In the end, neither side accepted the requests of the other and thus a full-scale war broke out between the Roman Republic and the Latin League.

The new conflict soon also involved the Samnites and the Campanians. The Samnites sided with Rome, hoping to obtain control of Capua in exchange for their military support, while the Campanians supported the Latins, hoping to free themselves from Roman rule now that the Samnite menace had temporarily vanished. The combined Latin-Campanian army did not attack Rome but moved into Samnium to raid the lands there. However, the Samnites opposed the invasion of their home territory by using guerrilla tactics, forcing the invaders to move south into the fertile plains of Campania. Here, a large Roman military force was waiting for them. The decisive battle of the campaign was fought near Vesuvius and ended with an overwhelming Roman victory. After this defeat the Campanians abandoned their allies, leaving the surviving Latins to march back north alone. Another battle was fought between the Romans and Latins in the territory of Latium Vetus shortly after these events, and again the Latin League forces were defeated.

During the following two years (339–338 BC) the Romans subjugated all the Latin cities one by one, attacking them with no mercy. In the end, the Latins had no choice but to surrender and all their cities were annexed by Rome (albeit in different ways, according to their past behaviours), with the Latin League formally abolished. Many Latin cities were annexed to the Roman Republic, while others were forced to become allies. Now the Romans could impose their will without having to discuss with a powerful confederation like the Latin League, which enabled them to have more direct control over the Latin cities. The Campanians and the city of Capua also became vassals of Rome due to the support they had given to the Latin rebellion. The Samnites, however, did not receive anything in exchange for the help they had given to the Romans. This snub was one of the main causes that led to the outbreak of the Second Samnite War in 326 BC.

Between the end of the hostilities with the Latins and the outbreak of the new conflict with the Samnites, the Roman Army was completely reformed. This was due to two main reasons: firstly, the Romans needed a much more flexible military machine in order to fight against new enemies who did not employ traditional hoplite tactics (like the Samnites and the Celts); secondly, with the inclusion of the Latins into the Roman Republic, the Romans could greatly expand their military forces by creating many new units of *socii* (allies).

The Romans abandoned their previous hoplite tactics and the army's general structure introduced by Servius Tullius. The tactical formations based on the deployment of the

Samnite/Lucanian warrior with Corinthian helmet and oval shield. (*Photo and copyright by Confraternita del Leone/Historia Viva*)

Samnite/Lucanian warrior with imported Thracian helmet. (*Photo and copyright by Confraternita del Leone/Historia Viva*)

phalanx on the open field had proved to be of very little use on the broken terrain of southern Italy, and had shown major deficiencies in terms of mobility. In order to fight and move more rapidly, the Roman legion had to be divided into smaller and more flexible sub-units, which could act as independent corps and operate not only in close formations but also as light infantry. To achieve this ambitious objective, the Romans decided to copy the best features of the Samnite military organization and introduce these in their own armed forces. The Samnite armies had always been structured on small units of sixty warriors each, called *manipuli* by the Romans: these corps, extremely flexible, were small enough to be assembled into larger formations but were also large enough to be employed in an autonomous way. Each *manipulus* could perform a specific task on the battlefield or garrison a specific location of the territory. In addition, all *manipuli* could easily be rotated during a battle in order to have fresh troops on the front line at every moment of the clash. All these things were impossible or very difficult to do with a legion made up of *centuriae*, which were too large to perform specific duties and were not trained to operate as independent corps. The great reform of the Roman Army that took place between the First and Second Samnite Wars is commonly known as the 'Manipular Reform', since it saw the rapid passage from a legion made up of *centuriae* to one comprising *manipuli*.

This transition was not easy to complete, largely because it took place together with a deep reform of Roman tactics and the adoption of new weapons for the whole Roman military machine. The Romans had understood that their subdivision of the infantry into five different 'classes' was completely outdated. The Samnites, for example, equipped all their warriors in a standard way as medium infantry that had javelins as their main weapons. The Roman heavy infantry hoplites were too slow to oppose the Samnite warriors on the open field and could use their traditional close formations only against the Etruscans or the Greeks who still fought in this 'old' way. The Roman light infantry of the lowest classes, meanwhile, had proven poorly equipped and trained when confronted by the Samnite skirmishers, who were armed with javelins but had helmet and armour. The Romans thus had to adopt new sets of equipment for their troops and replaced their hoplite spears with javelins. The original five 'classes' of infantrymen were transformed into three new categories of foot troops: the *hastati*, the *principes* and the *triarii*. According to this new system, the categories of troops were not created by assembling together soldiers from the same economic or social background, but by combining those of the same age and level of combat experience. The census was therefore no longer the key factor in determining the tactical function and personal equipment of each troop type.

The *hastati* were the youngest and least experienced soldiers of the army, with medium equipment in order to make good use of their agility. The *principes* were the

Gaul warriors equipped with spears and oval shields. (*Photo and copyright by Les Trimatrici*)

strongest and best-trained soldiers, receiving heavy equipment that also comprised javelins. The *triarii* were the oldest and most experienced veterans of the army, having heavy equipment that still included a hoplite spear. On most occasions, battles were fought only by the *hastati* and *principes*; there was no need to employ the *triarii*, who acted as a tactical reserve which was used only when absolutely needed. When the *hastati* and *principes* were routed, for example, the *triarii* were deployed in phalanx formation in order to create a screen behind which they could retreat. In general, due to their equipment – that included the hoplite spear – the *triarii* could perform only static or defensive duties and were not suited to offensive operations. They were the last remnants of the Servian phalanx and a symbol of Roman military pride: being a *triarius* meant you were a veteran who had been strong enough to survive at least a dozen battles. Each of the new Roman legions was to comprise a total of forty-five *manipuli*: fifteen of *hastati* who formed the first line, fifteen of *principes* who formed the second line and fifteen of *triarii* who formed the third line. As a result, in total, a manipular legion deployed some 2,700 medium/heavy infantrymen: 900 each of *hastati*, *principes* and *triarii*.

In addition to these, there were also another three categories of combatants that were included in the legion: the *leves*, the *accensi* and the *rorarii*. These all had light personal equipment and thus could not be deployed in close formation. The *leves* were the light equivalent of the *hastati* in terms of age and combat experience, and supported them in the first line; twenty *leves* were attached to each maniple of *hastati* and acted as explorers or skirmishers. The *accensi* and *rorarii* were the light equivalent of the *principes* and *triarii* regarding age and combat experience. Each *manipulus* of *triarii* was reinforced by one of *accensi* and one of *rorarii*. The *leves* were the vanguard of the legion, while the *accensi* and the *rorarii* supported the *triarii* in the rear of the formation. Each legion thus comprised 300 *leves* (twenty for each maniple of *hastati*), 900 *accensi* and 900 *rorarii*.

The transition from the Servian legion to the new manipular one happened as follows: the first three 'classes' of infantrymen were transformed into the *hastati*, *principes* and *triarii*; the Fourth Class was transformed into the *accensi*; and the Fifth Class became the *rorarii*. The *leves* were a brand new category of troops, which did not have its own separate *manipuli*. While the *accensi* and *rorarii* maintained the personal equipment that was characteristic of the classes from which they came, the leves received the lightest equipment of the whole Roman Army. It is clear that some distinctions related to the economic capabilities of each soldier continued to exist in the Roman Army: the rich citizens of the middle classes continued to serve in their own units, albeit now organized according to their age/combat experience; the poorer citizens still had their separate corps of light infantry (*leves*, *accensi* and *rorarii*).

To sum up, a manipular Roman legion comprised some 4,800 infantrymen organized into the following units: fifteen *manipuli* of eighty men each in the first line, fifteen of sixty men each in the second line and forty-five of sixty men each in the third line. As is made clear from the above, the rear of the legion comprised the largest number of soldiers who were all employed only in case of emergency, since the *accensi* and *rorarii* also made up a reserve like the heavily equipped *triarii*. At the back of the legion, the forty-five reserve maniples were deployed in three lines or *ordines*: first came the fifteen units of *triarii*, then the fifteen of *accensi* and finally the fifteen of *rorarii*.

The manipular reform also affected the organization of the cavalry. This now comprised 300 horsemen for each legion, structured on ten *turmae* with thirty soldiers each. As a result, the previous organization on *centuriae* was also abandoned for the cavalry. However, the cavalry continued to be made up of aristocrats and maintained its traditional panoply.

Gaul heavy infantryman with Montefortino helmet and chainmail. (*Photo and copyright by Confraternita del Leone / Historia Viva*)

Gaul warlord with Montefortino helmet and chainmail. (*Photo and copyright by Confraternita del Leone/ Historia Viva*)

After the end of the war against the Latins, around 335 BC, the Roman Army was greatly enlarged, with the previous two Servian legions transformed into four manipular legions. Each of the two consuls was to command a consular army with two legions, in order to avoid the danger of a single man controlling all the military power of Rome. Since each legion deployed some 4,800 infantry and 300 cavalry, a consular army had 9,600 foot soldiers and 600 horsemen. The whole Roman Army thus had 19,200 infantry and 1,200 cavalry.

However, the size of the army was supplemented by large contingents sent by the allies, who started to be organized in a much more stable and standardized way after the dissolution of the Latin League. Around 335 BC, all the allies of Rome were forced to adopt the manipular system and thus had to organize their own military forces in the new Roman way. The legions provided by the allies were commonly known as *alae sociorum* (wing companies), since they were deployed on the flanks of the Roman ones during battle. Their internal structure was slightly different from that of the Roman legions, since they contained a higher number of cavalry. Unlike the other Italic peoples, the Romans did not have a great cavalry tradition and preferred to fight as infantrymen. As a result, starting a trend that would continue until the mid-centuries of the Roman Empire, Roman commanders preferred to employ cavalry contingents almost entirely formed by allied soldiers. Each *ala sociorum* had 5,700 soldiers, with 4,800 infantry and 900 cavalry. The infantry were organized exactly like those of a Roman legion, while the cavalry were structured on thirty *turmae* with thirty horsemen each. By the time of the Second Samnite War, the allies of Rome had been organized into four *alae sociorum*, with two for each consular army. The *socii* of Rome thus provided an impressive force of 22,800 soldiers (19,200 infantry and 3,600 cavalry), giving Rome a total fighting force of 43,300, 4,800 of whom were mounted. On the battlefield, the soldiers of a consular army – 9,600 Roman infantry, 600 Roman cavalry, 9,600 allied infantry and 1,800 allied cavalry – were deployed as follows: the infantry of the two Roman legions was in the centre, with one *ala sociorum* on each flank; the Roman cavalry made up the first line of each wing, with ten *turmae* on each side, while the allied cavalry comprised the remaining three lines of each wing, each line having ten *turmae* of allied horsemen.

The Second Samnite War started in 326 BC after the Romans resumed their penetration of Campania by creating new settlements and confirming their alliances with the Campanians. The Samnites had been preparing for a new war for years and were ready to face the Romans in a large-scale conflict. The war began with a Roman invasion of Samnium, which obtained some good results in the early phases: several Samnite settlements located on the borders with Campania were occupied by Rome and the countryside surrounding these urban centres was looted by the Romans. There

Gaul standard-bearer with chainmail and oval shield. (*Photo and copyright by Confraternita del Leone/ Historia Viva*)

were no major military engagements in 325–324 BC, with the Roman Army unable to penetrate into the main Samnite territory and the Samnites adopting a defensive strategy to avoid a pitched battle with the more numerous enemy forces. In 323 BC the two sides concluded a temporary truce and during the following year a single clash was fought: this was not decisive and ended with a partial Roman victory. In 321 BC, after five years of inconclusive campaigning, the Romans decided that the time had finally come to deal with the Samnites once and for all. The Samnites' intelligent strategy had seen them avoiding a frontal clash with the Romans by remaining inside their territories, while at the same time damaging the Campanian allies of Rome by organizing small-scale raids and incursions. The Romans had no choice but to invade Samnium if they wanted to end the war and establish their prominence over the fertile plains of Campania.

The Romans assembled their forces in Capua and planned to march into the heart of Samnite territory, advancing towards the rich settlements of the Caudines, the most important of the Samnite tribes. The territory that the Roman Army had to cross, located on the border between Campania and Samnium, consisted of two consecutive valleys surrounded by mountains: the Suessola Valley and the Caudine Valley. The former had a very narrow entrance and was linked to the latter by a mountain pass. The Samnites did not attempt to block the Romans at the entrance of the Suessola Valley, preferring to deploy their forces on the mountains surrounding the valley. When the Romans reached the mountain pass that marked the entrance into the Caudine Valley, the Samnites acted rapidly to put in practice a plan they had elaborated to stop the Roman invasion. Part of their forces attacked the few Roman troops that had been left in the rear and gained control of the entrance of the Suessola Valley, while another part was deployed in the narrow mountain pass that marked the entrance of the Caudine Valley. Here the Samnites had built some very strong defensive positions, using trunks and stones to fortify the pass and make it impossible to assault. The Romans, who did not know the territory that they were crossing very well, were caught unawares. Upon reaching the mountain pass, they saw that the Samnites were waiting for them: after considering various options, the Roman commanders launched a frontal assault against the Samnite forces deployed in the pass. This was easily repulsed by the defenders, who caused serious losses to the Romans. As a result, realizing that the mountain pass was impossible to take, the Roman Army marched back to the entrance of the Suessola Valley, only to discover that the Samnites had occupied the other pass that connected the valley with the countryside of Capua and that this had been similarly fortified. As the Romans realized that they had been trapped in the valley, Samnite forces started to emerge from the woods of the mountains that surrounded the Suessola Valley. Several thousand Samnites stood ready to attack the invaders from their dominant positions,

Gaul warlord with Agen helmet and long sword. (*Photo and copyright by Les Trimatrici*)

using their javelins before launching a charge. At this point the Roman commanders had two alternatives: either they could fight and in all probability be massacred, since there was no hope of receiving reinforcements or supplies from Capua, or they could surrender in order to save their lives. The Romans decided to surrender: an entire army was captured by the Samnites. The Roman troops had to give up all their personal equipment and were left practically naked. In addition, they were forced to pass under the famous Caudine Forks under the hateful eyes of their Samnite enemies. The Caudine Forks consisted of three spears: two fixed vertically into the ground and one suspended horizontally between the other two; passing under them was a sign of humiliation and defeat, the like of which the Romans had never experienced before.

After such a crushing and humiliating defeat, Rome had to react quickly to maintain its dominance over Latium and Campania. In 320 BC, the Romans again marched towards Samnium and fought a pitched battle on the territory of the Caudines, winning a partial victory. A two-year truce was concluded between the warring sides in 318 BC, then in 315 BC the Romans obtained another indecisive victory at Saticula. Some months later the Samnites attempted an invasion of Latium, facing superior Roman forces in a pitched battle that ended without a clear winner. This clash, known as the Battle of Lautulae, was extremely hard-fought and caused severe losses to both sides. The Samnites launched an invasion of Campania the following year, but were defeated in battle by the Romans and had to retreat to their home territory. In 310 BC, with the Roman Army also fighting against the Etruscans on other fronts, the Samnites were able to secure a minor victory and seemed ready to resume their offensive towards Campania. In 308 BC, however, the Romans were able to deploy most of their forces in the south after crushing the Etruscan rebellion in the north, and went on to claim victory in a small-scale battle. During the following years both sides rebuilt their forces after their recent losses in preparation for a decisive campaign to end the conflict. In 305 BC, the Romans launched another invasion of Samnium: this time the operation was very well organized and planned, the Romans having acquired better knowledge of the enemy territory. The Samnites were unable to stop the advancing Romans as they had a few years before, and were forced to fight a pitched battle in order to defend their capital of Bovianum. The decisive clash took place not far from Bovianum and resulted in a clear victory for Rome. However, the Samnite forces had not been crushed and the Romans did not have enough men or resources to occupy Samnium. As a result, the two sides decided to end the conflict in 304 BC with the signing of a peace treaty, according to which the situation was restored to what it had been in 326 BC. Throughout two long and bloody wars, therefore, the Romans and Samnites had proved so equally matched that neither side had been able to permanently gain the upper hand.

Gaul warrior with Agen-Port helmet and chainmail. (*Photo and copyright by Les Ambiani*)

Between 304 and 298 BC, the Samnites tried to form a large anti-Roman alliance by convincing all the peoples of the Italian peninsula to join forces against their common enemy. The Samnites sent their envoys to the Etruscans, the Gauls and the Umbrians. The Etruscans had recently revolted against Rome and were still hoping to regain their independence, while the Gauls were extremely worried about Roman expansionism in Tuscany, since Rome's legions were coming nearer and nearer to their borders. The Umbrians, meanwhile, were one of the minor Italic peoples living in the centre of the peninsula and were the next target of the Romans. In the recent past these three peoples had fought against each other, but were now all determined to fight against Rome in order to defend their freedom. As a result, under the guidance of the Samnites, they put aside their differences and formed a single 'multi-national' army. The Romans, knowing full well that this new alliance would prove difficult to defeat, concluded their own new treaties with the Picentes and the Lucanians. The Picentes were a minor Italic people living on the northern borders of central Italy and had long been menaced by the Gauls, while the Lucanians were the main rivals of the Samnites in southern Italy. At the beginning of the new conflict in 298 BC, the Romans invaded Samnium and ravaged it on several occasions without encountering resistance, the Samnites having already transferred all their military forces to the north in order to form a single army with their new allies. After some minor clashes in Etruria, the decisive moment of the Third Samnite War came in the 295 BC, when at the Battle of Sentinum the Roman Army and the forces of the Italic league sponsored by the Samnites fought to the death. A total of some 60,000 Italic allies, mostly Celts and Samnites, were defeated by a combined military force of 38,000 Romans and Picentes. What became known as the 'Battle of the Nations' was a disaster for the Samnites and their allies, who lost around 25,000 men. After such a crushing defeat, the surviving Samnites fled to their home territory and attempted a desperate defence of Samnium. By 290 BC, the Romans had occupied most of the Samnite lands and were besieging the capital of Bovianum. The Samnites were eventually forced to surrender in order to save what remained of their homeland. However, their territory was greatly reduced and they were obliged to become allies of Rome. They retained some form of political independence, but had to renounce all their past ambitions and thereafter ceased to be serious rivals of Rome.

Chapter 6

The Pyrrhic War and the New Manipular Legion

By around 290 BC, Rome was already the leading power in central Italy and had more than one foothold in southern Italy. After the end of the bloody conflicts against the Samnites, the fertile plains of Campania were firmly under Roman control. At this point of their expansion, the Romans came into direct contact for the first time with the Greek communities of southern Italy. These were quite numerous and extremely rich: they had originally been founded as colonies of the great cities of Greece, but over time had become autonomous centres with their own political and military institutions. By 300 BC, while mainland Greece was under the control of the Macedonians, the Greek cities of Italy enjoyed a level of prosperity that was unrivalled in the Mediterranean. As a whole, these urban centres were known as Magna Grecia (Greater Greece), an expression that referred to those parts of the Greek world that were located outside mainland Greece. Thanks to commerce and agriculture, the cities of Magna Grecia had obtained control over large areas of southern Italy, in particular the coastline of the region. Their cities, with a few exceptions, were all important ports and had become rich thanks to naval trade. The Greek sphere of influence was, however, limited to the coastline. The interior of southern Italy, mostly covered with mountains, had never been penetrated by the Greek colonists and had always remained under control of the Oscan peoples (notably the Samnites, Lucanians and Bruttii) who had lived in the region for many years.

The defeat of the Samnites in 290 BC changed the political situation of southern Italy completely. Until then, the Greek cities had been in a state of indirect siege for many decades due to the expansionism of the Samnites and Lucanians. Now that the Samnites were no longer a menace, the Greeks could start planning to penetrate into the interior areas bordering their urban centres. It was clear to all the Greeks, however, that Rome was also ready to fill the gap left by the Samnites. Until that moment, the Romans had always fought against enemies with a civilization and culture that was comparable to their own. However, by fighting against the Greeks, they would face a new kind of enemy. The cities of the Magna Grecia were extremely strong from an economic point of view and had large fleets, but militarily only a couple of them could compare to Rome in terms of manpower. The leading cities of Magna Grecia were Syracuse in Sicily and Taras in southern Italy. In Sicily, the general situation of the

Gaul standard-bearer with 'parade' helmet and chainmail. (*Photo and copyright by Confraternita del Leone / Historia Viva*)

Epirote phalangites of Pyrrhus with their long spear (*sarissa*). (*Photo and copyright by Heitairoi*)

Greeks was quite different from that of the other Greek-speaking areas in Italy. Most of the extensive island was under Greek control, including the interior territories. Syracuse exerted direct control over most of Sicily, and by 290 BC had no rivals on the island except the Carthaginians. It should not be forgotten that before facing Rome, the Greeks of southern Italy had to fight against several other enemies to secure their positions. First they had to defeat the Etruscans, who wanted to extend their own commercial empire over the coasts of Campania and the central Mediterranean. After demolishing Etruscan naval power, the Greeks had to face the new menace represented by the Phoenician colonists of Carthage. The latter city, located not far from southern Italy in northern Africa, had ambitions to conquer Sicily and transform it into an advanced commercial base controlling the centre of the Mediterranean. While the Persians attacked the cities of mainland Greece, Syracuse had to repulse several Carthaginian attacks in Sicily. After decades of incessant warfare, the two warring sides found a temporary compromise: Carthage obtained control over western Sicily, while Syracuse retained its hegemony over the Greeks of central and eastern Sicily.

The situation of Taras (which the Romans later named Tarentum, the modern Taranto) was quite different from that of Syracuse. Until 290 BC, the Tarentines could exert their influence over a large part of continental southern Italy without having to fight any major war. While conflicts between Taras and the Oscan peoples were quite frequent, these were usually conducted on a very small scale and did not cause severe losses to the participants. This situation came to an abrupt end when Rome replaced the Samnites as the threat in the region and started to exert political pressure on Taras.

In 289 BC, the Lucanians and the Bruttii attacked the Greek city of Thurii in Calabria, taking advantage of some internal difficulties experienced by the Syracusans. The inhabitants of Thurii sent ambassadors to Taras seeking military support in their desperate struggle against the Lucanians, but returned empty-handed. At this point, firstly in 285 and then in 282 BC, Thurii asked for the military protection of Rome against the Oscans. The Roman Republic had finally found an opportunity to start playing a political role in Magna Grecia, presenting itself as the defender of Greek civilization from the attacks of the 'barbarian' Oscans. The Roman troops sent to Calabria in 282 BC were soon able to achieve a decisive victory over the Lucanians besieging Thurii, and as a result, several of the most important Greek cities in the region accepted Roman suzerainty in exchange for military protection. One of the urban centres that came under Roman influence was Rhegion, which had enormous strategic importance since it was located on the eastern side of the Strait of Messina. The strait connecting Sicily with mainland southern Italy is not far from Syracuse, and thus its possession was fundamental for every naval power who wanted to exert dominance over that part of the Mediterranean. After obtaining control of Rhegion,

Gaul warrior with Agen-Port helmet and leather armour. (*Photo and copyright by Contoutos Atrebates*)

Tarantine phalangite of the *Leukaspides* ('White Shields'). (*Photo and copyright by Heitairoi*)

the Romans sent a strong garrison of 4,000 soldiers to the city to defend it from any enemy attacks. As Syracuse and Taras could not accept that Rome was gradually replacing them as the leading power of southern Italy, they started planning a counter-offensive against Rome. Rome had recently concluded a treaty of alliance with Taras, according to which the Romans could move their land forces throughout mainland southern Italy but could not send their warships south of their own coast. Clearly, the Tarentines wanted to benefit as much as possible from their naval superiority and thus could not permit the arrival of Roman warships in their waters. The Romans had no problems in accepting these conditions, as at that time they did not have a proper military fleet and they could move their troops on land without serious difficulties (as they did during the campaign against the Lucanians).

During the closing months of 282 BC, tension between Rome and Taras escalated rapidly. In order to provoke the enemy and have a *casus belli*, the Romans sent a small fleet of ten warships into the Gulf of Taras. This act, which was a clear violation of the existing alliance treaty, was not acceptable for the Tarentines, who attacked the Roman fleet and destroyed it, sinking four Roman ships and capturing a fifth. At this point, understanding that their city was at war with Rome, the Tarentines acted rapidly and sent their army against Thurii to expel the Roman garrison. Thurii was conquered and sacked, while the Roman soldiers defending it were forced to abandon Calabria. Upon this, the Romans mobilized their army and moved south to besiege and conquer Taras. The Roman advance was unopposed, the Tarentines retreating behind the walls of their city. The Tarentines had the greatest port of continental Italy and thus, thanks to their naval supremacy, could import all the supplies they needed from abroad in case of siege. Potentially, Taras could resist a very long siege without suffering serious hardships. While the Romans devastated the countryside surrounding Taras, the Tarentines sent their ambassadors to mainland Greece in search of allies who could help them in the war against the Romans. In particular, the ambassadors of Taras went to the Kingdom of Epirus, located in the territory of modern Albania (on the northern borders of the Greek world) and ruled by the great Hellenistic warlord Pyrrhus. Epirus, due to its proximity to southern Italy, had always been interested in conquering this region. An Epirote king had sailed to Italy in 334 BC in order to defend the local Greek cities from attacks by the Lucanians and Bruttii, but this expedition had achieved very little. Now, with Pyrrhus in command, the Epirotes had a new opportunity to make inroads in Italy. The new monarch was a very ambitious one, with great military experience and clear plans for the future of his realm. Being a relative of Alexander the Great and having a great personal charisma, Pyrrhus seemed the ideal man who could unify Magna Grecia into a single state, also including Epirus.

The Epirote king landed near Taras in 280 BC at the head of 25,000 soldiers, including a good number of professional Macedonian phalangites (members of the Macedonian-

Celtic warlord from *Gallia Cisalpina*. The transverse crest on the helmet and the *linothorax* show a clear Roman military influence. (*Photo and copyright by Teuta Arverni*)

Epirote phalangite with Pilos helmet and *linothorax*. (*Photo and copyright by Heitairoi*)

Celtic warrior from *Gallia Cisalpina* with leather armour. He is transporting his personal equipment exactly like a Roman legionary. (*Photo and copyright by Teuta Arverni*)

Panoply of an Epirote phalangite from Pyrrhus' army. (*Photo and copyright by Heitairoi*)

style phalanx) and twenty war elephants. These forces were quite representative of the high level of complexity that had been reached by the Hellenistic armies after the death of Alexander the Great. The Romans had never faced such a 'modern' military force and had no idea what a Macedonian phalanx was. Until that moment, they had always fought against traditional phalanxes made up of hoplites. As for war elephants, fighting these mighty beasts was something completely new for the Romans, who had never even seen them before. After reaching Italy, Pyrrhus left a garrison of 3,000 picked soldiers inside Taras and then marched to fight against the Romans in a pitched battle. This took place at Heraclea, not far from Taras, where the Epirote king built his camp after seeing that the local plain was perfect for the deployment of his phalangites and war elephants. In the ensuing clash, the Romans maintained their positions for the whole day and repulsed all the furious assaults of the Epirote king's forces. By the end of the battle, however, the Roman Army was forced to retreat due to the heavy casualties suffered during the day, and thus Pyrrhus could claim victory. Despite being shocked by the elephants, the Romans had been able to fight on almost equal terms against the Macedonian phalangites. Some 7,000 Roman soldiers had died in the battle, but Pyrrhus had obtained the first of his famous 'Pyrrhic victories' at the cost of 4,000 excellent, irreplaceable soldiers. The Romans could easily make up their losses by using the contingents of Italic allies, while the Epirotes were in no economic and logistical condition to receive reinforcements from Greece. The victory at Heraclea did, however, have some positive consequences for Pyrrhus, since it convinced the three main peoples of southern Italy (the Apulians, Lucanians and Bruttii) to join their forces with those of the Epirotes. All the Greek cities of continental Italy, including those who had accepted Roman suzerainty, sided with Pyrrhus and expelled the Roman garrisons that controlled their territory. At this point of the war the Epirotes moved north against Latium, probably with the intention of besieging Rome. Pyrrhus, however, had no idea of the great military resources that the Romans could deploy on their home territory. He soon had to abandon his plans as it became clear to him that Latium would be impossible to conquer.

In this phase of the war, Rome received some decisive economic and logistical support from Carthage. The Phoenician city, at that time an ally of the Roman Republic, feared that Pyrrhus could sail to Sicily and move against its territories located in the western part of the island. In effect, the Epirote king had presented himself as the 'protector of all Greeks' and his main political goal was that of expelling both the Romans and the Carthaginians from the borders of Magna Grecia. To do this he formed alliances with Taras in southern Italy and Syracuse in Sicily. In 279 BC, at Asculum in Apulia, the Romans fought a second battle against Pyrrhus and were again defeated, but as on the previous occasion they inflicted heavy casualties on the enemy (some 3,500 men). At this point the Romans retreated to their home territories to recover from the recent losses, while Pyrrhus decided to move to Sicily in order to help Syracuse and expel the Carthaginians from the island. Between 278 and 276 BC, the Epirote monarch gained several clear victories in Sicily but was unable to expel the Carthaginians from their last and strongest fortified position on the island, the city of Lilybaeum. This city was besieged by the Greeks for several months, until Pyrrhus was forced to abandon Sicily due to discontent among some of his local allies who refused to feed his forces any longer. Meanwhile, the Romans had reconquered all their former positions in southern Italy and were now menacing Taras. If Taras was conquered by Rome, Pyrrhus would lose his main logistical base and thus the possibility to return home to Epirus. The decisive and final battle of the Pyrrhic War was fought at Maleventum, on Samnite territory, in 275 BC. During the course of the previous years of war in Italy, Pyrrhus

Celtic warrior from *Gallia Cisalpina* with padded armour. (*Photo and copyright by Teuta Arverni*)

Thracian (left) and Phrygian (right) helmets employed in Magna Grecia during the Hellenistic period. (*Photo and copyright by Heitairoi*)

had lost all his war elephants and most of his Macedonian phalangites; as a result, at Maleventum, he was soundly defeated and was left with no option but to return home to Epirus. Taras and the local Epirote garrison were then besieged for three years by the Romans, until the Greek city was finally conquered in 272 BC.

After their first encounters with the Hellenistic phalanx of Pyrrhus, the Romans understood that their manipular legion introduced during the period of the Samnite Wars was too 'light' to face a massive formation of well-trained heavy infantrymen on the open field. The manipular legion had been designed to fight against a highly mobile and lightly armed enemy like the Samnites, but the new enemies of the Romans were the Hellenistic armies of the East that all deployed phalangites among their many military contingents. As a result, in order to update their manipular legion, the Romans had to carry out another military reform. The first step of this was to increase the number of soldiers in each *manipulus* from sixty to 120, allowing the basic Roman unit to be large enough to face its equivalent in the Hellenistic phalanx (the *lochos* or 'company', comprising 128 heavy infantrymen). The internal structure of the light infantry contingents was also completely changed, with the three existing categories (*leves*, *accensi* and *rorarii*) abolished in order to create a single, unified light infantry corps:

Gaul warlord with Negau helmet and leather armour. (*Photo and copyright by Les Ambiani*)

Greek light infantryman with Pilos
helmet and javelins. (*Photo and
copyright by Heitairoi*)

the *velites*. As a result, the new manipular legion started to be deployed on three lines (*acies*) as follows: the first line was formed by ten *manipuli* of *hastati*, each supported by forty *velites*, for a total of 1,200 *hastati* and 400 *velites*; the second line comprised ten *manipuli* of *principes*, each supported by forty *velites*, for a total of 1,200 *principes* and 400 *velites*; while the third line was formed by ten *manipuli* of *triarii*, each supported by forty *velites*. The maniples of *triarii* remained of the old type with just sixty soldiers each and were not expanded to 120 men; as a result, the third line of a legion comprised only 600 *triarii* and 400 *velites*. In total, the infantry of a new manipular legion consisted of 4,200 men: 1,200 each of *velites*, *hastati* and *principes*, and 600 *triarii*. The proportions of heavy and light infantry had therefore greatly changed: in the previous version of the manipular legion there were 2,700 heavy infantry and 2,100 light infantry, whereas in the new one there were 3,000 heavy infantry and 1,200 light infantry. Light troops were fundamental for a campaign fought against the Oscan peoples on the broken terrain of Samnium, but were of little use against a Macedonian phalanx from Epirus.

In case of national emergency, as happened during the Second Punic War with Hannibal's invasion of Italy, the infantry of a legion could be expanded to 5,100 men: this was done by adding 300 soldiers to the first line of *hastati*, 300 to the second line of *principes* and 300 to the *velites* (100 for each of the three *acies*). Generally speaking, from a tactical point of view, the *velites* were of greatest use before and after a battle: before the clash they were tasked with explorative and skirmishing duties, while after it they could help the *triarii* in covering the retreat (in case of defeat) or attack the retreating enemy (in case of victory). During the battle itself, the light infantry simply initiated the clash by throwing their javelins and thus provoking the enemy, although on some occasions they could help their own cavalry against the mounted troops of the enemy or attack the flanks of war elephants. The Roman cavalry was not affected by the military reform described above, continuing to be organized on ten *turmae* with thirty men each for each legion. As a result, the new manipular legion had exactly 4,500 soldiers: 4,200 infantrymen and 300 cavalrymen. The *alae sociorum*, the allied legions, adopted the new organizational system introduced for the Roman Army, but continued to have 900 horsemen each instead of the standard 300. During the military emergency caused by the Epirote invasion of Italy, Rome mobilized all its available resources and was able to deploy in the field two consular armies, with six legions each: instead of the usual armies with two Roman and two allied legions, the Romans deployed consular armies with four Roman and two allied legions each. This meant that Rome could field two armies with 28,200 men each, for a total of 56,400 soldiers. These numbers were very impressive for the standards of the time, even for the largest Hellenistic armies. A new Mediterranean superpower had been born.

Gaul standard-bearer with 'parade' helmet and longsword. (*Photo and copyright by G.A.S.A.C.*)

The standard panoply of a Greek light skirmisher, comprising javelins and small round shield. (*Photo and copyright by Heitairoi*)

Tarantine light horseman with Sidon helmet and oval shield. (*Photo and copyright by Heitairoi*)

The basic panoply of a Tarantine light cavalryman, comprising a couple of javelins. (*Photo and copyright by Heitairoi*)

Chapter 7

The First Punic War and the
Conquest of Gallia Cisalpina

With the defeat of Pyrrhus and Taras, Rome had acquired control over all the continental territory of southern Italy. The Greek cities of the region were all forced to recognize the Romans as their formal 'protectors', while the local Oscan peoples (the Lucanians and the Bruttii) had to become *socii* of the Roman Republic. Since Etruria had already been conquered and the Picentes were already allies of Rome, we can say that most of the Italian peninsula was under Roman control. Only two areas were still independent: northern Italy (inhabited by several Celtic tribes) and the islands of Sicily, Sardinia and Corsica. The first target of the Romans, after conquering Taras in 272 BC, was Sicily, which was the most fertile region of Italy and produced large amounts of top-quality grain. In addition, thanks to its key location in the centre of the Mediterranean, it could be employed as a perfect base for further expansionist campaigns. From a political point of view, Sicily was extremely fragmented: the western part of the island was in the hands of the Carthaginians, who also controlled Sardinia and Corsica, while the centre and east of the island were ruled by Syracuse, which had gradually imposed its dominance over all the other Greek cities of Sicily.

As we have seen, the Carthaginians (called *Punici* by the Romans) and the Syracusans had been constantly at war against each other for many years. Since 289 BC, this difficult political situation had been further complicated by the appearance of a new local 'actor', the Mamertini. These were Italic mercenaries, mostly Oscans, who had been contracted by Syracuse to fight against the Carthaginians. At that time, as we will see, the Syracusan army was mostly composed of mercenaries from every corner of the Mediterranean; the Mamertini, whose name meant 'sons of Mars', were the most effective and violent of these. When in 289 BC the Syracusan tyrant who had contracted them died, the Mamertini became a problem for the new government of the city. They disbanded the large mercenary army that had been employed against the Carthaginians and paid off the Mamertini for their services. While marching back to their homeland, however, the Oscan mercenaries decided to remain in Sicily in order to create their own independent settlement on the island. They assaulted Messina and conquered it with a surprise attack, thus becoming rulers of the strait that separated mainland Italy from Sicily. The Mamertini quickly transformed themselves into pirates and started

Gaul warrior with Agen–Port helmet and leather cuirass. (*Photo and copyright by Les Mediomatrici*)

Warrior of the Bruttii, with Oscan standard and bronze war belt. (*Photo and copyright by Heitairoi*)

to attack all merchant ships passing through the Strait of Messina. This situation was obviously unacceptable for the Syracusans, who tried to destroy the Mamertini on several occasions but without success. When Pyrrhus came to Sicily during his Italian campaigns, the ex-mercenaries formed an alliance with the Carthaginians. In the following months they were defeated in battle on several occasions by the Epirotes,

The standard panoply employed by the Oscan peoples of southern Italy. (*Photo and copyright by Heitairoi*)

but they were able to retain control of Messina until Pyrrhus was forced to leave Sicily. In the years following the defeat of Pyrrhus, the Mamertini continued to be supported by the Carthaginians and became even stronger. Soon after the departure of the Epirotes, the city of Rhegion came under the control of the former mercenaries. During the war against Pyrrhus, the Romans had garrisoned Rhegion with a legion of allies formed by Campanians as the city was located in front of Messina on mainland Italy, and thus controlled the other side of the strait. After the Epirotes abandoned Sicily, the Campanian legionaries revolted against Rome and killed their officers. They proclaimed the independence of Rhegion and formed an alliance with their Oscan 'brothers' in Messina. As a result of these events, the Mamertini had formed a piratical kingdom that was centred around the Strait of Messina. In 270 BC, the Romans decided to intervene and sent an army against Rhegion, which was besieged and retaken with the help of Syracuse. At this point the Romans could have sent their troops to Sicily to help the Syracusans against the Mamertini in Messina, but since the city was located outside mainland Italy the Roman intervention would have represented a violation of the treaty between the Romans and Carthaginians, under which Sicily fell into Carthage's sphere of influence.

During the following years the Syracusans tried to defeat the Mamertini alone, and they secured a clear victory over their ex-mercenaries in 265 BC. At this point, being on

Lightly armed warrior from *Gallia Cisalpina*. (*Photo and copyright by Teuta Arverni*)

the verge of destruction, the Oscan pirates formally requested Carthaginian military help. The Carthaginians sent a fleet and installed a small garrison in Messina, as a result of which the Syracusans, being in no condition to fight alone against Carthage in a new war, suspended their military operations against the Mamertines. At this point, however, Rome decided to intervene in Sicily by 'using' the Mamertines to prevent the Carthaginians from gaining complete control over the Strait of Messina. In 264 BC, using as *casus belli* the request for help sent by some Mamertines who were hostile to the Carthaginians, Rome sent an army against Messina and thus initiated the First Punic War against Carthage. The Romans easily crushed the Mamertines and occupied Messina before the Carthaginians could react, meaning they now controlled both sides of the strait and had an important base from which to conquer the rest of Sicily. Fearing that most of their territory could be soon occupied by the Romans, the Syracusans chose to ally themselves with their former Carthaginian enemies. Before the Carthaginians and Syracusans could join forces, the Romans defeated the Syracusan Army and then moved against the Carthaginian force that was marching against Messina. After also defeating the Carthaginians, the Romans secured their control over Messina and then started besieging Syracuse. On the verge of defeat, Syracuse concluded a truce with the Romans in order to preserve its independence. At this point, using the resources of their new allies, the Romans moved to conquer central Sicily. The Carthaginians assembled most of their forces at the strategically important city of Agrigento, which was besieged for seven months by the Romans before being conquered in 261 BC.

At this point of the First Punic War the Romans had won a series of clear victories on land, but the Carthaginians were still the masters of the Mediterranean Sea. Until that time Rome had never had a proper military fleet, being able to deploy only a very limited number of small warships. The landing in Sicily had been possible only thanks to the decisive naval support received from the allied Greek cities of southern Italy, which gave the Roman military forces in Sicily all the logistic support they needed. If the Romans wanted to defeat the Carthaginians at sea, however, they needed to have their own fleet. However, this was not so easy to achieve, for several reasons. First of all, building an entirely new fleet from scratch and in a short time had enormous costs. The Romans also had no experience of naval combat and knew practically nothing of Carthaginian tactics. Finally, the Romans did not have any naval bases, and thus depended on their Greek allies for construction and repair of the warships. Despite all these problems, the Roman Republic was able to build a fleet of 120 warships in the Greek naval arsenals of southern Italy and to train 30,000 Italic peasants as sailors in just a few months. The first naval battle between Romans and Carthaginians took place at the Aeolian Islands in 260 BC and was a defeat for Rome. After this initial failure,

Celtic warlord from northern Italy. The influence of the Italic peoples is clearly visible in the clothes and jewels. (*Photo and copyright by Teuta Arverni*)

Oscan warrior of the Mamertini wearing a bronze *cardiophylax* (rectangular plate) for protection of the chest. (*Photo and copyright by Heitairoi*)

however, the Romans rapidly learned from experience and were able to defeat the Carthaginians at Milazzo. The Roman success was determined by the use of the *corvus*, a new boarding device that was unknown to the Carthaginians and which consisted of a mobile wooden bridge with a heavy spike on the underside. By using the *corvus* the Romans could easily stop and board a Carthaginian warship, thus transforming a naval clash into a land battle during which the legionaries could employ their superior weapons and tactics. After obtaining their first naval victory, the Romans also sent troops to Sardinia and Corsica, expanding the conflict to the whole central part of the Mediterranean. In 257 BC, with a new and larger fleet, the Romans tried to end the war by invading North Africa with an army of 97,000 soldiers. The Carthaginians attempted to prevent the invasion by assembling a fleet of 250 warships with 150,000 men. In the ensuing Battle of Cape Ecnomus, the greatest naval clash of Antiquity, the Romans obtained a clear victory and destroyed most of the enemy vessels. After disembarking in Africa, the Roman army obtained some minor victories and threatened Carthage. At this point the hostilities were temporarily suspended to allow peace negotiations, but the talks produced no results. When hostilities were resumed, the Carthaginians restructured their land forces in Africa by putting them under the command of a mercenary Spartan general named Xanthippus. He completely reorganized the Carthaginian Army along Hellenistic lines in a very short time, and was able to rout the Romans at the Battle of Tunis in 255 BC. The few surviving Roman soldiers were forced to abandon North Africa, but during the journey back to Sicily the entire Roman fleet was destroyed by a terrible storm. The Romans made another attempt to disembark their troops in Africa in 253 BC, but again the campaign was a failure and the fleet was destroyed by a storm while sailing back to Sicily.

The situation of the field armies in Sicily had not changed much since the early moves of the war, with the Romans controlling the eastern portion and the Carthaginians the western one. In 249 BC, the Roman fleet, which had been rebuilt, was destroyed by Carthage at the Battle of Trapani, after which there were no major battles on land or at sea for six years as both Rome and Carthage had employed all their available resources. The Romans were finally able to build a new fleet in 242 BC, and during the following year they won a decisive victory over the Carthaginian navy at the Battle of the Aegades Islands. This clash marked the end of the First Punic War, since Carthage was in no condition to continue the fight. The subsequent peace treaty heavily favoured Rome, with the Carthaginians forced to evacuate Sicily and pay an immense war indemnity.

During the following years the Carthaginian state went bankrupt due to the financial burden caused by payment of the war indemnity. This had very negative consequences for the Carthaginian empire in the Mediterranean, since there was not enough money to build new warships or to pay the thousands of mercenaries who made up the Carthaginian armies. The mercenaries revolted against their masters

Gaul heavy infantryman with Montefortino helmet and chainmail. (*Photo and copyright by Confraternita del Leone / Historia Viva*)

Oscan warrior of the Mamertini equipped with the small shield and long spear that were typical of Hellenistic phalangites. These elements were the result of the Mamertini's long period of service in the Syracusan Army. (*Photo and copyright by Heitairoi*)

and ravaged most of present-day Tunisia before being defeated by the Carthaginians. This episode, known as the 'Revolt of the Mercenaries', had important consequences for the islands of the western Mediterranean. With the Carthaginians temporarily without a fleet and the city of Carthage menaced by the mercenaries, the Romans were left free to transform Sicily into their first province and send military expeditions to the other islands. According to the peace treaty, Sicily was to remain as a neutral zone between the Roman and Carthaginian possessions. However, after the Carthaginians abandoned the island, the Romans occupied most of it except for Syracuse, which was transformed into a Roman protectorate. Upon the outbreak of the Second Punic War, Syracuse would revolt against the Romans, only to be conquered and annexed to the Roman province of Sicily.

In Sardinia and Corsica, the situation was somewhat different at the end of the First Punic War. The local Carthaginian garrisons, which had not been defeated by the Romans during the course of the war, were entirely made up of mercenaries. When these were not paid by Carthage at the end of the hostilities, they revolted – like their comrades in North Africa – and devastated much of the area where they were garrisoned. Taking advantage of this situation, presenting itself as the defender of the local Sardinian and Corsican peoples, Rome sent military expeditions to both islands and transformed them into a new province after defeating the mercenaries. By 227 BC, both Sardinia and Corsica were under the firm control of Rome, despite sporadic rebellions by the local population. During the Second Punic War, the Sardinians revolted against Rome and obtained some great military victories, but these last serious attempts at rebellion were eventually crushed by the Roman legions.

With the events of the First Punic War, Rome had transformed itself from a regional power into a Mediterranean one. The only part of Italy that was still free from its rule was the vast northern area dominated by the Celtic tribes. In 249 BC, the Celts of Cisalpine Gaul ('Gaul south of the Alps'), under strong Roman pressure and hoping to take advantage of the ongoing conflict between Rome and Carthage, decided to ask for help against Rome from their 'cousins' of Transalpine Gaul ('Gaul north of the Alps'). The Celts from present-day France, being in search of new lands due to overpopulation, gave a positive response to this request and sent a large army into northern Italy. According to ancient sources, this comprised 50,000 foot warriors and 25,000 horsemen. Thanks to these new resources, the Italian Celts were able to resume hostilities against the Roman Republic. We have no precise details about these 75,000 warriors who marched south towards Italy, although ancient writers call them Gaesatae, using a term that probably meant 'mercenaries' in the Celtic language. This would seem to confirm that the Gaesatae were not migrating to Italy with their families and goods, but rather were warriors who had been recruited by Cisalpine emissaries.

Gaul light skirmisher equipped with javelins. (*Photo and copyright by Contoutos Atrebates*)

Gaul light infantryman equipped with javelins. (*Photo and copyright by Les Ambiani*)

The population of Transalpine Gaul was increasing greatly at this time, so there were too few resources to sustain such a large number of inhabitants. Minor warlords and young warriors were in search of new opportunities and new lands because their home territory had little to offer them. The 75,000 mercenaries from north of the Alps appeared more 'barbarian' to the Romans than those living in northern Italy because they had experienced very little contact with the Mediterranean world and thus had preserved their original Celtic identity.

The Republic was surprised by the arrival of such a strong military force from Gaul and initially had serious problems in containing the Celts. Hostilities between the Romans and Gauls lasted for many years, until 225 BC, during which time the Gaesatae proved to be excellent warriors and defeated the Republic on several occasions. In 225 BC, however, a decisive clash was fought at Telamon between the Romans and the Celts. Like at Sentinum seventy years before, the battle ended in complete disaster for the Gauls, who suffered enormous losses. The military potential of the Gaesatae had been broken, but the same could not be said of the Cisalpine Gauls' spirit. In 223 BC, in a bid to finally crush their resistance, the Romans sent an army of 40,000 soldiers to invade northern Italy. The campaign was successful from the beginning, helped by some Celtic tribes deciding to side with Rome, hoping thereby to acquire some new lands. During the following year another large battle was fought between Romans and Gauls at Clastidium, which again resulted in defeat for the Cisalpine Celts, and thus their whole territory in northern Italy was occupied by Rome, including the important centre of Mediolanum. Cisalpine Gaul had fallen and the Romans were now masters of the whole Italian peninsula. The Celts, however, had only surrendered because they had no more resources to continue the fight. At the first opportunity they revolted against Rome in order to regain their freedom, which happened in 218 BC when the Second Punic War broke out between Carthage and Rome. After joining Hannibal and making up a good portion of his forces when he invaded Rome, the Italian Celts were left alone when the Carthaginian general finally left Italy in 202 BC. Two years later, at the Battle of Cremona, the Celts were crushed by the legions. This clash proved decisive for Cisalpine Gaul: although some fighting continued until 194 BC, the Celts could no longer contest Roman dominance over their lands in northern Italy.

Chapter 8

The Etruscans

Over the centuries many theories regarding the origins of the Etruscans have been proposed by scholars, but none of these has been accepted as the 'definitive' one by the international scientific community. Three theories have become the most popular: the first, based on Herodotus, considers the Etruscans as an Asiatic people coming to Italy during the thirteenth century BC from Anatolia; the second, based on Dionysius of Halicarnassus, considers the Etruscans as the only 'indigenous' Italic people who survived the migrations of the Indo-Europeans into the Italian peninsula; the third, based on Livy, considers the Etruscans as one of the many Indo-European peoples who invaded Italy in two waves before the twelfth century BC. Considering various elements and bearing in mind that the Etruscans were quite different from all the other peoples living in the Italian peninsula before the ascendancy of Rome, the first of these theories seems to me to be the correct one. During the thirteenth–twelfth centuries BC, Italy was invaded by a great number of Indo-European tribes from the heart of Central Europe. These peoples, with their superior civilization, easily defeated the indigenous populations of the peninsula and colonized every corner of Italian territory. It was during this historical phase, for example, that the Latins came to the region where Rome would be built. Later, several decades after these events, a second wave of Indo-Europeans came to the Italian peninsula: these comprised the warlike Oscan peoples like the Samnites, whose arrival caused a revolution in the political stability of ancient Italy. Between these two waves of Indo-European migration, the Etruscans started to develop their own civilization in present-day Tuscany. If we compare their way of life with that of the Indo-European peoples, we can clearly see that the Etruscans had quite little in common with the communities living around them: they had a different language, a different religion and a different way of life. For these reasons, the theory based on the scripts of Livy seems to be inaccurate if we judge according to archaeological sources. The same could be said for the theory based on the scripts by Dionysius of Halicarnassus. Indeed, since the very early stages of their civilization, the Etruscans had a very complex culture that can't be compared with the simple way of life practised by the indigenous peoples living in Italy before the thirteenth century BC. As a result, considering that the Etruscans have much in common with the peoples of ancient Anatolia from a cultural point of view, the theory initiated by Herodotus seems to be the most correct one.

Celtic standard-bearer from *Gallia Cisalpina. (Photo and copyright by Les Ambiani)*

Syracusan naval hoplite wearing Attic helmet and no armour. (*Photo and copyright by Athenea Prómakhos*)

Around the twelfth century BC, present-day western Turkey was devastated by a series of unexpected events that led to the collapse of the Mycenean and Hittite civilizations. These events, of which we know very little, included invasions by warlike peoples and several natural disasters. These were probably the cause of the mass migrations that took place between the end of the Bronze Age and the beginning of the Iron Age. In any case, it was during this complex historical phase that the Etruscans started to develop their own civilization in Tuscany. According to Herodotus, they came from Anatolia and their migration to Italy was caused by a terrible famine which affected that part of Asia. After arriving in Italy, the Etruscans occupied Tuscany but continued to expand north (towards the Po River valley) and south (along the fertile coastline of Campania). This first phase of Etruscan civilization is commonly known as the 'Villanovian' one, which coincided with their expansion in Italy and lasted until the eighth century BC. It was at the end of this historical phase that the city of Rome was founded and that the Greeks started to colonize southern Italy, thus initiating a new 'age' for the civilizations of ancient Italy. One of the key factors that made the Etruscans different from the other Italic peoples was their capability to build excellent ships and practise commerce over long distances. With the arrival of the Greeks, however, the Etruscans had for the first time to face a rival naval power, and this changed the balance of power in the central part of the Mediterranean. During the seventh–sixth centuries BC, the Etruscan civilization underwent a deep transformation – commonly known as 'orientalization' – which saw the adoption of many Greek practices like phalangite military tactics. It was during this period that the Etruscans imposed their control over Rome, but the political situation of Italy soon started to change.

By the seventh century BC, the original agricultural Etruscan villages of the Villanovian period had transformed themselves into city-states, populated by artisans and merchants who were growing rich thanks to commerce. Each urban centre was independent and had its own king, who was generally assisted by an assembly of rich citizens who made up the nobility. Like in early Rome, the economic position of a citizen generally corresponded to his social place. Over time, similarly to what happened in Rome, some Etruscan cities abandoned monarchy as their form of government and started to elect a couple of magistrates on a yearly basis instead of choosing a monarch. However, power remained in the hands of the assembly, which was formed by the wealthiest citizens. During the period of the three Etruscan kings, Rome was heavily influenced by the Etruscan civilization and adopted many of its distinctive features: the use of a written alphabet, the practice of predicting the future by reading from the intestines of sacrificed animals or by interpreting the flight of the birds, staged fights between gladiators, the use of the *fasci littori* as a symbol of power and the practice of building arches to celebrate military victories. Twelve of

Gaul military musician with *carnyx* horn.
(*Photo and copyright by Les Ambiani*)

Syracusan naval hoplite wearing Chalcidian helmet and no armour. (*Photo and copyright by Athenea Prómakhos*)

Gaul warlord with chainmail and *carnyx* horn. (*Photo and copyright by Confraternita del Leone/Historia Viva*)

the Etruscan cities became particularly prominent and thus formed a military alliance known as the Etruscan League or Dodecapoli: Arezzo, Caere, Clusium, Cortona, Perugia, Populonia, Tarquinia, Veii, Vetulonia, Volsinii, Volterra and Vulci. When the Etruscans reached the zenith of their territorial expansion, they controlled a good part of eastern Corsica and had a strong naval base in Naples. During the sixth century BC, however, a series of defeats marked the beginning of the end for Etruscan military power. In central Italy, Rome became independent from Etruscan influence and initiated a series of wars against Veii. In northern Italy, all the Etruscan settlements of the Po Valley were conquered by Celtic newcomers, while in southern Italy and the central Mediterranean Sea, the Greeks started to replace the Etruscans as the leading commercial power. In 540 BC, at the Battle of Alalia, the Etruscan fleet (allied with the Carthaginians) was defeated by the Greeks from Cuma. This naval clash marked a real turning point in the history of the Etruscans and was the beginning of a long decline. In 309 BC, at the Battle of Lake Vadimone, the Etruscans suffered their last crushing defeat at the hands of the Romans. Although some years later they took part in the bloody Battle of Sentinum (see Chapter 5), their destiny was by now decided.

During the sixth century BC, Etruscan cities adopted the military organization that was later introduced in Rome with the Servian reforms. According to the sources, there was only one difference between the military structure of Etruscan cities and that of Rome: in the Etruscan urban centres, the infantry of the army was organized on four classes and thus there was no Fifth Class. In addition, the Etruscan Fourth Class had a different internal composition compared with the Roman one, comprising both light infantry (equipped with bows or javelins) and heavily equipped axemen (chosen soldiers). The latter were a real peculiarity of the Etruscans: equipped with double-edged axes, they had a very precise tactical function on the battlefield, that of breaking the shield wall of the enemy phalanxes by using their two-handed weapons. The presence of axemen in a phalangite army is something that we find only in the Etruscan military system, and is a clear sign that all the Etruscan cities had armies organized according to the contemporary Greek models (since axemen could be employed with success only against close formations of hoplites). The Etruscan axemen operated together with the hoplites of the First Class, since they had no shield for personal protection. Their equipment was the same as the heavy infantry, but they wore a single greave instead of two (in order to have a better degree of mobility, the greave was on the leg that was put forward while using the axe). Differently from the Romans, whose entire cavalry had heavy equipment, the Etruscans also deployed some contingents of lightly armed mounted troops. In general, the Etruscan light troops – be they foot or horse – were usually provided by their allies or were recruited from mercenaries. On many occasions, thanks to their great economic resources, the Etruscans could employ large numbers of mercenaries on the battlefield.

Gaul heavy infantryman with
Montefortino helmet and
chainmail. (*Photo and copyright by
Antichi Popoli*)

Syracusan *hamippos* armed with javelins and short sword. (*Photo and copyright by Athenea Prómakhos*)

Chapter 9

The Latins and the Peoples of Central Italy

Under the famous 'seven kings', the Romans fought dozens of wars against the other peoples who lived in the territory of Latium Vetus. These peoples had different military traditions and experienced different relationships with the emerging city of Rome. Broadly speaking, it is possible to divide the peoples of ancient Latium into two main categories: the first comprises the populations that arrived in central Italy with the first wave of Indo-Europeans; the second comprises those that settled in Latium as part of the second wave of Indo-Europeans. The first group included the Latins, Falisci and Capenati, while the second group had the Oscan peoples of the Sabines, Equi, Volsci, Ernici and Aurunci. Initially the Latins lived in small agricultural communities consisting of small fortified settlements, known as *oppida*. Over time, however, some of these centres started to become proper cities and assumed a more prominent political role. The new Latin cities soon began forming military and religious leagues between themselves in order to have a common defence policy in case of enemy attack and to reinforce the traditional cultural ties existing between them. The most important of these leagues was that guided by Alba Longa, the richest of all the Latin cities. Later, as we have seen, all the Latin urban centres formed a Latin League, which was initially dominated by the Romans but later abolished when the Roman Republic decided to absorb all the Latin territories. After submitting to Rome, the Latins became the most important allies of the Republic and contributed decisively to all the victories obtained by the Romans in Italy (during most of the period investigated here, the *alae sociorum* were essentially Latin legions).

The Falisci and the Capenati lived in northern Latium, in that part of the region north of the Tiber which soon came under strong Etruscan political influence. Both peoples were loyal allies of Veii for most of their history, and thus followed the destiny of the great Etruscan city when the latter was conquered by the Romans after a long siege. Of the three major Oscan peoples of Latium (the Sabines, Equi and Volsci), we have already said a lot regarding their numerous wars against Rome. As we have seen, the Equi and Volsci were strongly linked by a series of cultural and political ties, fighting together as allies against Rome on many occasions. The Equi lived in the mountainous terrain of eastern Latium, while the Volsci inhabited a vast marshland situated in the southern part of the region. The Sabines had been one of three original communities that had created the city of Rome and, at least until the ascendancy of the Etruscan kings, had exerted a strong political influence over the newly founded city. Over time, however, they were cornered by the Romans in the Apennine mountains and suffered a series of defeats. On several occasions they formed military alliances with the other Oscan peoples, but they were the first to be defeated and absorbed into the Roman Republic. The Ernici and Aurunci were two minor participants in the great 'political game' of Latium, since their military resources were not comparable to those of the other Oscan peoples. The Ernici, who were organized into a league, inhabited a small territory located between the lands of the Equi and those of the Volsci. They were loyal allies of the Romans until 508 BC, but when Rome became a republic they joined forces with the other Oscan peoples until being defeated and conquered in 306 BC. The Aurunci lived on the southern borders of Latium, with the Volsci to the north and the Campanians to the south. They had five major urban centres and were always loyal allies of the Volsci. When the Volsci were defeated, they found a new ally in the Samnites (their home territory bordered Samnium in the east). At the end of the Second Samnite War, as a consequence of their support for the Samnites, the Aurunci were absorbed into the Roman Republic. From a military point of view, the peoples of Latium were organized in different ways. The Latins, who were from the beginning strongly influenced by the Romans, adopted the phalangite military system shortly after Servius Tullius introduced it in Rome. The Falisci and the Capenati continued to fight as light infantrymen until being conquered by the Romans, and usually provided the light contingents to the Etruscan armies operating around Veii. The Oscan peoples, meanwhile, retained their traditional way of fighting based on guerrilla warfare and fast incursions until being conquered.

In addition to the Etruscans and the peoples of Latium, central Italy was also inhabited by other populations living on the eastern side of the peninsula. The eastern portion of central Italy was covered by high mountains and thus did not have the natural resources that were needed for the development of a great civilization. It was, however, inhabited by several warlike peoples who had a lot in common with the Equi and the Samnites. In the south, in the eastern region corresponding to Latium on the other side of the Apennines, there were the Marsi mountain dwellers; in the north, in the eastern region corresponding to Etruria across the Apennines, there were the Picentes; and between Etruria and the Picentes there were the densely forested lands inhabited by the Umbrians. Generally speaking, these three peoples were extremely warlike, being of Oscan stock, but were conquered quite easily by the Romans. The Marsi, semi-nomad shepherds who were used to very harsh conditions, lived in the most isolated area of the Italian peninsula and thus had little contacts with the rest of the world. They consisted of three tribes: the Marrucini, the Peligni and the Vestini.

Syracusan hoplite with
Chalcidian helmet and
composite cuirass. (*Photo
and copyright by Athenea
Prómakhos*)

Syracusan hoplite with Corinthian helmet and *linothorax*. (*Photo and copyright by Athenea Prómakhos*)

Syracusan hoplite with crested Corinthian helmet. (*Photo and copyright by Athenea Prómakhos*)

Syracusan hoplite with pseudo–Attic helmet and leather armour. (*Photo and copyright by Athenea Prómakhos*)

Until 325 BC, these communities remained quiet, playing no role in the wars fought by the expanding Romans. In that year, however, Rome decided to launch a pre-emptive invasion against the Marsi in order to prevent them forming a military alliance with the Samnites (something that was seen as probable but not yet certain). After suffering several defeats and putting up a strong resistance on their mountains, the Marsi concluded a peace treaty with Rome, according to which they promised to remain neutral in the wars between Rome and the Samnites. In 301 BC, however, the Marsi rose up against the Romans to regain their independence. They were defeated in battle, but put up a strong resistance in their mountains until finally being overwhelmed. Subsequently, they became one of Rome's most trusted allies.

Before the emergence of the Etruscans, the Umbrians had dominated a large portion of Italy that was known as Great Umbria, comprising Tuscany and the southern portion of the Po Valley. With the arrival of the Etruscans and the later invasions of the Celts, the Umbrians were forced to abandon most of their homeland and became a secondary power of central Italy. When the menace represented by the Gauls became more serious, the Umbrians formed an alliance with the Etruscans in a bid to stop the expansionism of the newcomers. In 295 BC, however, they decided to join the Celts as well as the other Italic peoples at the Battle of Sentinum. The Romans largely campaigned that year with the intention of conquering Umbria, which had a strategic location connecting the Etruscan territories with those of the Celts and Samnites. With the defeat at Sentinum, the Umbrians lost their independence forever and were forced to become allies of Rome. The Picentes, famous as craftsmen and merchants, occupied a large portion of central Italy that connected the Celtic lands in the north to those of the Marsi in the south. The arrival of the Gauls in the Po Valley marked the beginning of a new phase in their history, the newcomers occupying a good portion of the original homeland inhabited by the Picentes. The Picentes, however, were able to retain their independence and continued to fight against the Celts for decades. In 299 BC, the Picentes concluded an anti-Celtic alliance with the Romans and fought with them during the decisive Battle of Sentinum. In 269 BC, unhappy at their alliance with Rome, the Picentes rebelled against the Romans and fought two campaigns against their former allies. Eventually, however, their territory was also annexed by the Roman Republic. From a military point of view, the Marsi and the Picentes had much in common with the Equi and the Samnites, while the Umbrians were heavily influenced by the Etruscans but also (in later times) by the Gauls.

Chapter 10

The Gauls and the Peoples of Northern Italy

During the historical period analysed in this book, northern Italy was inhabited by three different peoples: the Ligures in the west, the Celts/Gauls in the centre and the Veneti in the east. We have already said a lot about the Gauls in the previous chapters, so here we will give some more details about the other two peoples who lived around their territories. The Ligures were probably the first Indo-Europeans to settle in the peninsula, since they arrived in Italy around 2,000 BC. It would be wrong to consider the Ligures only as an Italic people, because initially they lived across a vast territory that comprised most of present-day southern France as well as the entire western portion of northern Italy. During the thirteenth century BC, when new Indo-European communities arrived in Italy, the Ligures lost most of their original lands and were confined to a small strip along the coastline of north-west Italy. Since those days, this region has been known as Liguria, which is mostly covered with broken and hilly terrain, thus not very suited for agriculture. The Ligures gradually transformed themselves into a 'pirate people', making a living thanks to naval incursions. They became famous throughout the Mediterranean for their great seafaring capabilities, and also started to be employed as mercenary warriors by several military powers of Antiquity. The Ligures fought as unarmoured light skirmishers and were very capable naval infantry. Being used to very harsh conditions, they could endure any kind of physical privation. With the arrival of the Celts, the Ligures lost some of their home territory and had to fight for survival against the newcomers. However, the Gauls and Ligures eventually started to live together without any major problems. As a result, a new 'mixed' culture appeared in the western part of northern Italy which contained both Celtic and Ligurian elements.

When the Romans conquered Etruria, the Ligures acquired a common border with the expanding Republic. Rome understood the strategic importance of Liguria, a small region with few natural resources but one that connected Italy with the rest of Western Europe, most notably with Gaul. During the First Punic War the Romans tried to conclude several treaties of alliance with the Ligurian tribes, but all their attempts came to nothing. The Ligures had long provided large numbers of mercenary warriors to the Carthaginians, and continued to do so during the conflict fought by Carthage against Rome. During 238 BC, in response to the hostile behaviour of the Ligures, the

Gaul heavy infantryman equipped with sword and leather greaves. (*Photo and copyright by Antichi Popoli*)

Romans launched an invasion of Liguria. On land, thanks to massive support from the Celts, the Ligures were able to resist by using guerrilla tactics, which were perfectly suited to the broken terrain on which they lived. At sea, however, the Ligurian fleet was completely destroyed by the Romans. With the outbreak of the Second Punic War, some Ligurian tribes fought on Rome's side but the majority joined Hannibal in his invasion of Italy. When the Carthaginians abandoned the peninsula, the Romans occupied Liguria with strong military forces, but the Ligures were able to put up a ferocious resistance thanks to the support that they continued to receive from Carthage. During the period from 197–155 BC, they fought against the Romans by using hit-and-run tactics, obtaining some local successes. The Ligures retreated back to the most inhospitable hills and mountains of their homeland, where it was practically impossible to find them without running the risk of being ambushed. More than 50,000 Ligurian prisoners were taken by the Romans and moved to other areas of Italy in a bid to bring the guerrilla war to an end. In the long run these harsh methods of repression worked, with all the Ligurian tribes gradually forced to surrender. By 155 BC, Liguria was under full Roman control and was used by the expanding Republic as its main base for operations directed against southern Gaul.

The Veneti were an Indo-European people and arrived in Italy around the end of the Bronze Age. They came from the ancient region of Illyria, corresponding to the western part of the Balkans. They soon started to develop a flourishing civilization, based on commerce: their products, such as vases, were of top quality and were exported to several areas of Italy. The Veneti had very good relations with the Etruscans of the Po Valley and were not a warlike people. They were strongly influenced by the Villanovan culture of the Etruscans and exerted control over vast areas of north-eastern Italy. Like the Ligures they had great seafaring capabilities, and thus were able to create important commercial routes that connected Central Europe with the Balkans in the east and Italy in the west. Unlike most of the other Italic peoples, from 800 BC the Veneti started to live in large urban settlements and adopted some forms of modern social structure. Each city had its own monarch and was fully autonomous from the others: from this point of view, the Veneti had a lot in common with the Etruscans. With the arrival of the Celts, the Veneti had to renounce most of their territories and were gradually absorbed by the newcomers. Like with the Ligures, a new 'mixed' culture emerged in the territory of the Veneti, who had no choice but to accept the Celtic presence.

In 283 BC, the Veneti signed an important treaty of alliance with Rome. Like the Picentes who lived on their southern borders, they considered Rome the only military power that could defeat the Gauls. After the Romans overcame the Gauls, the Veneti remained loyal allies of the Republic for the rest of their history and were gradually absorbed by the Romans. During the sixth century BC, the Veneti adopted a military organization that was quite similar to the contemporary Etruscan one, based on classes of equipment that derived from the social/economic position of each warrior. The Veneti had four classes of warriors in their armies: the First Class was equipped with an oval shield, spear with a butt spike and helmet; the Second Class was equipped with a rectangular shield, spear without butt spike and helmet; the Third Class was equipped with a round shield, spear without butt spike and helmet; and the Fourth Class was equipped with a single-handed axe and helmet. Clearly, the Third Class of the Veneti corresponded to the hoplites of the Etruscan First Class, the First Class of the Veneti to the Second Class of the Etruscans and the Second Class of the Veneti to the Third Class of the Etruscans. The axemen of the Veneti, meanwhile, made up the same Fourth Class as the Etruscans. Judging from contemporary sources, the Veneti deployed their classes of infantry in a peculiar way, with the hoplites making up the third line behind the other two classes equipped with oval and rectangular shields. This different tactical pattern was probably a result of the strong military influence that the Celts had over the Veneti. They also had some cavalry, which had the same light equipment as the infantry's Fourth Class.

The military organization of the Gauls did not change much during the period taken into account, since Celtic armies were never structured on regular military units like the Greek phalanxes or Roman legions. Military contingents were raised according to their tribal or familial origins, being strongly linked to the clan to which they belonged. When the leader of a Celtic tribe decided to go to war, all the free men living under his protection had to serve, the farmer-warriors leaving their homes and assembling at the hill fort of their warlord. Some military leaders were powerful and rich enough to be named kings and thus controlled very large territories. In cases of war, all the minor aristocrats living on the land of these kings had to assemble their tribal contingents and join their overlord to form a 'royal' army. Celtic military organization was based on the solid personal relationships existing between the upper class of the nobles and the large community of peasants and farmers. For raids or incursions against bordering tribes, free men could decide to join their warlord with the hope of looting the enemy's resources, but they were not obliged to abandon their farms. However, if there was a full-scale foreign invasion or large expedition of conquest, all able-bodied free individuals were obliged to fight. Celtic military organization was not so different from that of later Feudal Europe: an army was formed from several different contingents, each led by a noble warlord who commanded his own personal retainers. A certain number of the latter could be professional fighters who earned a living as soldiers, but the majority were part-time warriors who had to serve in exchange for protection and benefits. Each warlord commanded a different number of warriors and there were no

Gaul slinger; his only personal protection is a Montefortino helmet. (*Photo and copyright by Antichi Popoli*)

standard tactical units: a great noble could assemble thousands of men, while a minor one might lead into battle just a few hundred followers. The overall commander of a Celtic army, which could be a king or simply the most prominent warlord, usually experienced serious problems in keeping together so many military leaders and their warriors. Celtic cavalry was formed from the nobles and included both war chariots and individual horsemen, while the infantry comprised all the free men of a community.

Chapter 11

The Samnites and the Peoples of Southern Italy

As we have already seen, the Samnites were among the deadliest enemies of the Romans, their great military capabilities obliging Rome to reform its military forces by adopting the new manipular system. The Samnites were masters of 'transhumance', a semi-nomadic pastoralism that was practised along the Apennines and which characterized the economy and society of several Italic peoples. By moving across the mountains of central and southern Italy with their livestock, they knew about all the inland routes and the most important passes, so unlike the sedentary peoples living around them, the Samnites could easily move and transport most of their goods and thus were very difficult to defeat by using traditional warfare tactics. They were known as 'lovers of freedom' by all the other Italic peoples, and were also famous for their austere way of life. A Samnite boy was used to fighting against his enemies from childhood in order to defend his sheep from raiders or wild animals. The small villages of the Samnites were usually built near important mountain passes or rivers, since control of the land routes and of the natural resources was fundamental for the inhabitants of Samnium.

The Samnites comprised four different tribes: the Caudini, who lived in the area of present-day Benevento; the Irpini, who lived around present-day Avellino; the Pentri, who lived in the southern half of Molise; and the Carricini, who lived in the northern half of Molise. There was also another minor tribe, that of the Frentani, who lived between the Marsi in the north and the Samnites in the south, but had much more in common with the latter. The four main tribes made up the Samnite League, which was expanded with the inclusion of the Frentani by the time of the Samnite Wars. After the end of the wars, despite having been defeated, the Samnites rebelled against the Romans on several occasions and caused some serious problems for the Republic. When Pyrrhus and Hannibal invaded Italy, the warlike Oscans from Samnium joined the armies fighting against Rome and provided thousands of excellent warriors to the Epirote and Carthaginian forces. On both occasions, however, the defeat of the invaders resulted in harsh repressions for the Italic peoples who had abandoned Rome. Many Samnite villages were destroyed and thousands of civilians from Samnium transferred by the Romans to other parts of Italy.

The Samnite Army was structured on *manipuli* of 200 men each, which were usually assembled in pairs and thus on most occasions the basic Samnite unit comprised 400

Greek hoplite with Chalcidian helmet and *linothorax*. (*Photo and copyright by Athenea Prómakhos*)

Greek hoplite with Corinthian helmet and 'muscle' cuirass. (*Photo and copyright by Athenea Prómakhos*)

warriors. Each *cohors* – or couple of *manipuli* – was deployed on two lines: the first comprised warriors equipped with javelins, while the second had warriors armed with spears. Apparently there was no difference in the equipment carried by the various maniples, since all Samnite fighters had several javelins and one spear as their main offensive weapons. When deployed in battle, however, the members of a *cohors'* first line were required to use their throwing weapons, while those of the second line had to adopt a more static formation by employing their spears. In practice, the second line had to cover the retreat of the first in case of defeat or had to advance in close formation in case of success. If needed, a single *manipulus* could be broken into two *centuriae* of 100 men each in order to have a higher degree of mobility on broken terrain.

In addition to the regular *manipuli*, the Samnite Army also included a very large special corps known as the *Legio Linteata*. This chosen unit, comprising only veteran warriors with much combat experience, totalled some 16,000 men and thus made up a fundamental part of the Samnite Army. The members of the *Legio Linteata* had publicly devoted their lives to the main gods of Samnite religion, according to a practice known as *devotio*, in which a sacred oath was made inside a special fence which had a roof made of linen (hence the adjective *linteata*). Upon becoming a member of this corps, a Samnite warrior would serve his gods and his community as a soldier for the rest of his life. Cowardice and desertion were punished with immediate death: if one of their comrades betrayed the homeland, the members of the *Legio Linteata* could kill him without prosecution. Executions were conducted in front of the community, in order to show everyone the rigidity of Samnite military discipline. According to contemporary sources, the *Legio Linteata* was a permanent military unit and thus also served full-time in peacetime. Differently from the rest of the Samnite Army, which was mobilized only in case of war, this chosen unit was made up of professional soldiers with superior training. The warriors of the *Legio Linteata* mostly came from the most prominent families of Samnium and had their own peculiar equipment, which comprised silver helmet and armour. Their tunics and shields were white, with the result that it could be easily distinguished from other Samnite units. From an organizational point of view, this special corps was divided into ten sub-units of 1,600 men each, which comprised four *cohortes* of 400 warriors each. As a result, the *Legio Linteata* had more or less the numerical consistency of a Roman consular army with four legions. On the field of battle it was deployed on the right of the Samnite Army.

As we have seen, the Greeks started to colonize the coasts of southern Italy during the eighth century BC and founded several cities in the region. During the following decades, the Greek communities in the peninsula began flourishing and became a significant commercial power. The interior of southern Italy, however, was never colonized by the Greeks due to strong resistance by the local Oscan peoples: these,

Greek hoplite with Corinthian helmet and composite cuirass. (*Photo and copyright by Athenea Prómakhos*)

Greek hoplite with Attic helmet and 'muscle' cuirass. (*Photo and copyright by Heitairoi*)

similarly to the Samnites, represented a strong military menace for the Greeks until Rome conquered the urban centres of Magna Grecia. Basically, there were three Oscan peoples in southern Italy (in addition to the Samnites): the Campanians, Lucanians and Bruttii. In addition to these, that part of the peninsula was inhabited by another Indo-European population whose origins can be traced back to the southern Balkans and whose culture was similar to that of the Illyrians: the Apulians or Iapygians, who lived in present-day Puglia. The Campanians lived in one of the most fertile regions of Italy, known as *Campania Felix*, and were famous for their excellent cavalry, who were considered to be the best in the peninsula. They inhabited several smaller centres but also the major city of Capua, which until the Punic Wars had roughly the same demographic and economic importance as Rome. With the arrival of the Greeks and the emergence of the Etruscans, the Campanians had to renounce most of their coastal territories, which were occupied by the newcomers. The Campanians did not have a fleet and thus could do little to repulse the seaborne incursions. During the fifth century BC, however, they organized a massive counter-offensive against the Greeks and Etruscans. The city of Cuma, the most important Greek urban centre in Campania, was reoccupied in 421 BC, and thereafter the Etruscan strongholds around Naples were conquered. This 'renaissance' of the Campanians, however, did not last long due to the ascendancy of the Samnites, who were intent on conquering *Campania Felix*. As we have seen, the possession of Capua was a main cause of the First Samnite War, after which the Campanians and their main city became one of Rome's most trusted allies and provided a lot of manpower for the *alae sociorum*. During the Second Punic War, the Campanians rebelled against Rome and joined the Carthaginians, transforming Capua into the main base of Hannibal. With Carthage's defeat, however, the Campanian territory was reconquered by the Romans and lost any kind of autonomy.

The Lucanians lived in the interior of southern Italy south of Samnium. They had for many years tried to limit the expansion of the Greek colonies, and were seen as their mortal enemies. On several occasions the Lucanians were victorious against these 'foreigners', for example besieging and conquering some of their most important urban centres. This was the case with present-day Paestum, which was founded by the Greeks and later occupied by the Lucanians. Judging from contemporary sources, the Lucanian warriors fought exactly like the Samnites, like whom they could move very rapidly through the mountainous terrain of the Apennines. Around the beginning of the fourth century BC, the Lucanians formed a strong military alliance with the Greek city of Syracuse, the dominant power of Sicily which was keen to damage its rival Greek cities in mainland southern Italy. Since they had an enemy in common, the Lucanians and the Syracusans collaborated on several occasions and gained some important victories. Thanks to the help received from Syracuse, the Lucanians

Apulian warrior with Italo-
Corinthian helmet and 'muscle'
cuirass. The general appearance
of this fighter shows the strong
influence exerted by the Greeks of
Taras over the Apulians. (*Photo and
copyright by Heitairoi*)

Detail of the Italo-Corinthian helmet worn by an Apulian warrior. (*Photo and copyright by Heitairoi*)

conquered most of present-day Calabria and thus reached the southern tip of mainland Italy. At this point the Syracusans started to change their opinion about the Lucanians, realizing that they could soon become a threat to their hegemony over Sicily. Trying to limit the power of their former allies, the Syracusans fomented a revolt among the slaves of the Lucanians, who during their recent campaigns had captured thousands of enemies but were too few to control them. This civil war had a devastating effect on the Lucanians, since it produced a new population, the Bruttii, former slaves who had revolted against their masters and became independent from the Lucanians. The Bruttii quickly occupied all the Calabrian lands that had been recently conquered by the Lucanians.

After the violent secession, the Lucanians continued their long struggle against the Greek cities of southern Italy and attacked Taras, menacing it on several occasions. To resist, the Tarantines had no choice but to ask for military help from their motherland, Sparta, which sent some troops to fight against the Lucanians. Later, in 323 BC, the Tarantines had to ask for help again in order to repulse a new Lucanian offensive, and this time they received support from Alexander I of Epirus, uncle of Alexander the Great and predecessor of Pyrrhus. The first Epirote campaign in southern Italy, however, was a failure: fearing that the newcomers could remain in Italy, the Lucanians and the Bruttii concluded a treaty of alliance and joined forces to defeat Alexander I (who died in combat during the expedition). One generation later, as we have seen, the Lucanians joined forces with the Epirote Army and fought under command of Pyrrhus as part of a large alliance that also comprised the Bruttii and the city of Taras. When Taras was defeated by the Romans, the Lucanians were forced to become allies of the Republic. Like the Samnites, however, they soon started preparing for a revolt against their conquerors. The opportunity to do so came with the arrival of Hannibal in Italy, but when the Carthaginians were defeated the Lucanians were punished harshly by the Romans, as were all the Italic peoples who had rebelled. After becoming an independent people, the Bruttii started to live as mountain-dwellers and shepherds in the Apennines of Calabria. Here they built several small villages, which were united in a confederation known as the *Confoederatio Bruttiorum* and having as its capital Consentia, the only major city of the Bruttii. After joining Pyrrhus and being defeated, the Bruttii followed the same destiny as the Lucanians: they supported Hannibal during the Second Punic War, but after the victory of the Roman Republic they had no choice but to submit to Rome.

The Apulians lived in present-day Puglia, a region of southern Italy where the territory consists almost entirely of fertile plains and which also included the important city of Taras. Thanks to their excellent agricultural production, notably grain, the Apulians had become rich and their civilization was one of the most flourishing in

Hoplite equipment, including Chalcidian helmet and composite cuirass. (*Photo and copyright by Athenea Prómakhos*)

Italy. They were Indo-Europeans of Illyrian stock, originating from the southern part of the Balkans. After crossing the Adriatic they settled in Puglia and established themselves in their new territory according to their tribal organization. The Apulians comprised three main communities: the Dauni, who settled in northern Puglia; the Peucezi, who settled in central Puglia; the Messapi, who settled in southern Puglia. The Apulians built several rural settlements in their new homeland and became famous for the quality of their horses, comparable in Italy only to those of the Campanians. With the ascendancy of Taras, the three Apulian tribes started to experience a series of problems. The Dauni started to be heavily influenced by the Samnites, who lived on their western borders, and thus acquired several features that were typical of the Oscans. With the arrival of Alexander I of Epirus, however, they were partly overrun by Taras and asked for military help from Rome in order to regain their independence. The Dauni concluded a treaty with the Romans in 327 BC, siding with them during most subsequent conflicts. In the Second Punic War, however, they abandoned Rome

Warrior of the Apulians (left) and warrior of the Bruttii (right). (*Photo and copyright by Heitairoi*)

Warrior of the Bruttii equipped with Phrygian helmet and trilobate cuirass. (*Photo and copyright by Heitairoi*)

and joined forces with Hannibal. After the latter's defeat, the northern part of Puglia was occupied by the Romans in 194 BC. The Peucezi and the Messapi, bordering with Taras, formed a military alliance in order to stop the expansion of the Greek colony. In 473 BC, thanks to the superiority of their cavalry, they obtained a great victory over the Tarantines. During the following decades, with substantial support from the Lucanians, they continued to attack the territory of Taras. With the arrival of Alexander I of Epirus, however, the Peucezi and the Messapi were finally defeated and submitted to the Tarantines. As allies of Taras they took part in the campaigns of Pyrrhus, but when he was defeated by the Romans their territory was conquered by the Republic.

Chapter 12

The Greeks and the Insular Peoples

The Greeks started to colonize Italy during the eighth century BC as a result of the demographic boom that was affecting their home territories, which obliged many communities to leave mainland Greece in search of new lands to settle. With Italy being an extremely fertile land adjacent to the western Greek coast, it soon became the most important destination for all the emigrants from the various cities of Greece. After several decades, the Greek colonies of Italy started to flourish and became even richer than most of the cities in mainland Greece, having more natural resources at their disposal and thus being able to enlarge their population without limits. Two cities

Hoplite equipment, including Corinthian helmet and *linothorax*. (*Photo and copyright by Athenea Prómakhos*)

founded by the Greek colonists, Taras and Syracuse, came to dominate *Magna Grecia* and later challenged Rome for possession of strategic lands.

Taras, Sparta's only overseas colony, was founded in 706 BC. Unlike many of the Greek colonies in Italy, the city had a solid democratic constitution (introduced in 473 BC) that provided a high degree of internal stability. From a military point of view, the Tarantines were more or less the Italic equivalent of the Thessalians in Greece: controlling much of Apulia's extensive plains, Taras could deploy large numbers of excellent cavalry (mostly having light equipment). Over the years the Tarantine horsemen started to be employed as mercenaries in every corner of the Hellenic world, and thus acquired a great military reputation. When we speak of 'Tarantine' light cavalry, we should bear in mind that this indicates horsemen from Taras only for the Classical period; during the later Hellenistic period, the term 'Tarantine' started to indicate all mercenaries (mostly Greek) equipped like the original light cavalrymen from Taras. The adjective 'Tarantine' thus no longer bore a geographical significance but was used purely as a tactical term to indicate a precise category of troops. 'Tarantine' horsemen were light skirmishers equipped similarly to the Thessalians, but in addition to the traditional javelins they also carried a helmet and shield (which could be round

Hoplite equipment, including Attic helmet and 'muscle' cuirass. (*Photo and copyright by Heitairoi*)

Greek light infantryman from Magna Grecia with *pelte* shield and javelins. (*Photo and copyright by Athenea Prómakhos*)

or oval). They were a new category of medium cavalry, with no armour but with some capabilities to conduct close combat (thanks to the use of helmet and shield). They could act both as simple skirmishers and as 'shock' cavalry, albeit with minor impact compared with the Macedonian heavy cavalry.

The army of Taras comprised a phalanx of 20,000 men, 3,000 light cavalry of the kind described above and 1,000 heavy cavalry. The Tarantine phalangites were all equipped with white metal shields, and thus were commonly known as *Leukaspides* ('White Shields'). It is highly probable that it was Alexander I of Epirus who re-equipped the Tarantine traditional hoplites as phalangites and gave them their white shields during his ill-fated Italian campaign. The 1,000 heavy cavalrymen were known as *hipparchoi* and formed a separate unit from the light horsemen, being considered the real elite of the Tarantine Army. Thanks to their great economic resources derived from trade, the Tarantines could supplement their forces with large numbers of mercenaries, which could be either Greek (mostly Spartans) or Italic (from the same tribes that fought against Taras).

The Greek colonies in Sicily were even richer than those in mainland southern Italy, but had to face an enemy that was much more powerful than the Italic tribes. Since 734 BC, the Phoenicians had started to found their own colonies in the western part of the island. When these came under the political leadership of Carthage, Syracuse and the other Greek cities fought several wars against them in order to limit their expansionist ambitions. It soon became clear that Carthage wanted to conquer the whole of Sicily to control the most important commercial sea routes of the Mediterranean. Syracuse, being the most important and richest of the Greek colonies on the island, was the main target of the Carthaginians. The city had been founded by the Corinthians in 733 BC, and soon became very large. Due to the constant menace of foreign invaders, during the period we take into account Syracuse was mostly ruled by tyrants and only had very short periods of democratic government. Tyrants were the only political representatives powerful enough to counter the Carthaginians. One of the most important battles fought by the Syracusans against the Carthaginians was at Himera in 480 BC, which ended with a great victory for the Greeks of Sicily. The Carthaginians, however, were not the only enemies of Syracuse: in 415 BC, during the Peloponnesian War, the Athenians organized a massive naval expedition with the objective of conquering Sicily. Against all odds, the Syracusans were able to prevail in the ensuing campaign and captured thousands of Athenian soldiers, who were put to work as slaves for the remainder of their lives in the great Syracusan mines. The two most successful tyrants of Syracuse were Agathokles (who ruled from 317–289 BC) and Hieron (who ruled from 270–215 BC). Both tried to expand the power of the city over the other Greek colonies of Sicily, while at the same time opposing the Carthaginians.

Tarantine archer wearing the characteristic sun hat of the Thessalians. (*Photo and copyright by Athenea Prómakhos*)

While Syracuse acted as an ally of Rome during the First Punic War, during the Second Punic War the city sided with Carthage and was finally conquered by the Romans in 212 BC after an epic siege (during which the war machines created by the famous Syracusan inventor Archimedes caused serious difficulties to the attackers).

The Syracusan Army was mostly composed of mercenaries by the beginning of the Hellenistic period, the former citizen-soldiers who had defeated the Athenians during the Peloponnesian War having become only a distant memory. Due to their increasing wealth derived from commerce, the tyrants of Syracuse preferred recruiting impressive bodies of mercenaries instead of obliging their citizens to serve (that could cause the outbreak of revolts). This started to happen on a regular basis from the reign of Dionysius I (405–367 BC). Syracuse, thanks to its superior economic capabilities, was the only Greek colony of Sicily that could maintain an entire army of mercenaries. Therefore, similarly to the Carthaginians, the Syracusans recruited the best mercenaries of the western Mediterranean from a wide variety of sources. The mercenaries paid by Syracuse usually served in distinct units formed according to their nationality; they were commanded by their own officers and were equipped in their native style. At the time of Agathokles, the Syracusan Army on campaign could field the following troops: 3,500 Syracusan hoplites, 2,500 allied hoplites (sent by other Greek cities of Sicily), 1,000 chosen mercenary hoplites (Greeks who formed Agathokles' personal guard), 1,000 Samnite mercenaries, 1,000 Etruscan mercenaries, 1,000 Gallic mercenaries, 500 missile troops (archers or slingers) and 800 cavalry. With these impressive forces, Agathokles even managed to launch a military campaign in North Africa in an attempt to conquer Carthage. In many respects, the Syracusan Army was a private military force (*hetairia*) serving the tyrant who was currently in power. Its core was represented by the 1,000 chosen mercenaries, a permanent corps of professional soldiers who served under every tyrant. Mercenaries also came from other sources and could include the following: Cretan archers, Sicels (Italic native inhabitants of Sicily), Iberians (formerly in the service of Carthage), Ligurians and other Oscans (Lucanians and Bruttii). The Oscans, in particular, were known for their incredible valour and great cruelty. Many of them, at the end of their period of service, decided to remain in Sicily and thus formed their own settlements (a sort of military colony). Like the Tarantines, who invented a new category of light cavalrymen, the Syracusans created a new troop type during our period: the *Hamippoi*, introduced by Gelon of Syracuse and later exported to mainland Greece before the Peloponnesian War.

The Syracusan Army contained a good number of cavalry. These, in contrast to what happened in Greece, were more important than the hoplites and were an elite force. During the period 490–480 BC, the Greeks of Sicily fought a deadly war against the

Various models of Greek swords for the infantry; those with a curved blade are of the *kopis* type, while those with a straight blade are of the *xiphos* type. (*Photo and copyright by Athenea Prómakhos*)

Carthaginians, during which, in order to support his numerous horsemen against the Carthaginian heavy cavalry, Gelon created a new category of light infantrymen initially known as *Hippodromoi Psiloi*, or '*Psiloi* who run alongside the cavalry'. These, who would later become simply known as *Hamippoi*, were *Psiloi* (light infantrymen) with specific equipment and training. This derived from their peculiar tactical function: they had to go into battle running behind the cavalry, holding on to the tails or manes of the horses. In battle they slipped underneath the horses of the enemy cavalry and ripped their bellies open. As a result, they were equipped with a short dagger to stab the enemy mounts and were trained to run for long distances with the cavalry. Like all *Psiloi*, they had no body armour and simply wore a felt hat. In theory, each cavalryman should have been supported by one *Hamippos*, but this only rarely happened.

Before the arrival of the Greeks and Carthaginians, Sicily was inhabited by two Italic peoples: the Sicanians and the Sicels. The first of these had lived on the island for centuries, while the others reached it as part of the many Indo-European peoples who later migrated into Italy. The Sicels were more warlike than the Sicanians, and thus soon reduced the territory of the latter to a few internal areas of Sicily (mostly covered with hills). The progressive fusion between the Greeks and the Sicanians/Sicels was initially a peaceful one, but around the fifth century BC the indigenous peoples of Sicily revolted against the Greeks, guided by a great war leader known as Ducetius, who was able to obtain several victories. The revolt began in 461 BC and ended only eleven years later, when a Greek coalition headed by Syracuse gained the upper hand and Ducetius

Greek swords for the infantry, of the *xiphos* (left) and *kopis* (right) types. The latter model was particularly popular among the Italic peoples. (*Photo and copyright by Heitairoi*)

was forced to go into exile. After these events, Sicily remained under control of the Greeks until the outbreak of the First Punic War.

The situation in Sardinia was somewhat different, as since 1,600 BC the local population had developed a very advanced culture known as the Nuragic civilization (from the *nuraghe*, massive towers that were built in great numbers in every corner of Sardinia). The Sardinians lived in isolated settlements that were essentially villages. They were all shepherds and their economy was a very simple one. However, they could work the metals found on the island very well and had important commercial contacts with other peoples of the Mediterranean. Around the ninth century BC, the

Map showing the peoples of southern Italy and the location of the most important Greek colonies.

first Phoenician colonists reached Sardinia and started to build some outposts along the coast. Like the Etruscans in Corsica, the Phoenicians wanted to use Sardinia as an important base for their naval activities. When the various Phoenician settlements on the island came under control of Carthage, the foreign presence in Sardinia became much more significant. The Carthaginians discovered that Sardinia was full of potential mines, and thus tried to penetrate into the interior of the island. However, they met with strong resistance from local warriors, who had a very warlike nature and were equipped with good quality weapons. The broken terrain of Sardinia, having no roads and being covered by hills, was perfect to organize a strong resistance using guerrilla tactics. The Carthaginians landed a large army on the island in 535 BC, but in twenty-five years of skirmishes and ambushes they were only able to conquer the south-western portion of Sardinia. In the following decades, the Sardinians revolted on several

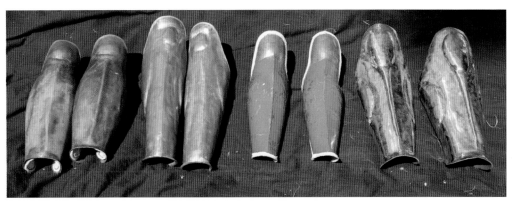

Various models of bronze greaves used by the hoplites of Magna Grecia. (*Photo and copyright by Heitairoi*)

Map showing Sardinia before the First Punic War; the areas marked in yellow were under direct Carthaginian control. (*CC BY-SA 3.0, Wikimedia User Xoil*)

Hoplites from the Greek colonies of southern Italy. (*Photo and copyright by Athenea Prómakhos*)

occasions due to the imposition of high taxation and because the Carthaginians used them as slaves to extract natural resources from the mines. By the outbreak of the First Punic War, the part of Sardinia that was under Carthaginian control had developed a distinctive civilization comprising both Punic and local elements. As we have seen, the Romans arrived in Sardinia after the island's Carthaginian garrison of mercenaries mutinied. The Sardinians resisted against the Romans, exactly as they had against the Carthaginians. In 215 BC, under the guidance of the great warlord Ampsicora, the whole population rebelled and attacked the Roman occupiers. Rome was at this time experiencing serious military difficulties against Hannibal in Italy and thus could not send reinforcements to Sardinia. The Carthaginians, however, landed 15,000 soldiers on the island to support the rebellion. Despite this, Ampsicora was defeated by the Romans in the decisive and bloody Battle of Decimomannu, which marked the end of the Carthaginian presence in Sardinia. The local population continued for decades to wage a terrible guerrilla war against the Romans, retaining control of all the island's interior, which started to be known as the *Barbagia* ('land of the barbarians'). The Romans enslaved thousands of Sardinians and transferred them to mainland Italy with the hope of crushing the resistance, but it was only in 111 BC that the island was finally pacified.

Conclusion

The Roman conquest of Italy was a long and difficult process, which shaped the destiny of Rome and changed the history of the Mediterranean world forever. At the beginning of this process the Romans were just a small community with the main ambition of just surviving, but over time they understood that Latium and central Italy could come under their control. From the beginning, Rome paid great attention to military matters and developed an excellent military organization; this greatly expanded across the centuries and had a very interesting evolution. After a first phase characterized by a strong Etruscan and Greek influence, the Roman Army introduced a new structure, based on the legions, that was extremely innovative for its time. This great change was the result of the conflicts fought by the Romans against the Samnites, who already had a flexible military organization that was quite different from the dominant one of the Greeks (based on hoplite warfare). By defeating the Greeks in southern Italy and the Celts in northern Italy, the Roman Republic unified the Italic peoples into a single state and started to expand in the central Mediterranean. Thanks to the hard lessons learned during the wars fought against Epirus and Carthage, the Romans would transform their military forces into a perfect combat machine that had no rivals in the known world. It is important to remember, however, that many key aspects of the Roman military had already been introduced by some Italic peoples before the Romans. The future glory of the Roman Empire, in fact, was based on a vast Italic heritage that the Romans could never ignore. Across the centuries, Etruscan culture, Samnite warfare, Greek art and Celtic weaponry were all adopted by the Romans and became an intimate part of their identity. During the Empire, these elements were exported across the Mediterranean and greatly contributed to the formation of Western Civilization.

Tarantine heavy horseman with Attic-
Boeotian helmet and scale armour.
(*Photo and copyright by Heitairoi*)

The standard panoply of a Tarantine heavy cavalryman, comprising a heavy spear in addition to the oval shield. (*Photo and copyright by Heitairoi*)

Bibliography

Primary sources
Diodorus Siculus, *History*
Herodotus, *The Histories*
Livy, *History of Rome from its Foundation*
Plutarch, *Lives*
Polybius, *The Histories*
Strabo, *Geography*
Thucydides, *History of the Peloponnesian War*

Secondary sources
Allen, S., *Celtic Warrior 300 BC–AD 100* (Osprey Publishing, 2001)
Canales, C., *El Ejército de Anibal* (Andrea Press, 2005)
Connolly, P., *Hannibal and the Enemies of Rome* (Silver Burdett Press, 1979)
Connolly, P., *Greece and Rome at War* (Frontline Books, 2016)
D'Amato, R., *Roman Centurions 753–31 BC* (Osprey Publishing, 2011)
Fields, N., *Carthaginian Warrior 264–146 BC* (Osprey Publishing, 2010)
Fields, N., *Early Roman Warrior 753–321 BC* (Osprey Publishing, 2011)
Fields, N., *Roman Republican Legionary 298–105 BC* (Osprey Publishing, 2012)
Fossati, I., *Gli eserciti etruschi* (Editrice Militare Italiana, 1987)
Head, D., *Armies of the Macedonian and Punic Wars 359 BC to 146 BC* (Wargames Research Group, 1982)
Kiley, K.F., *An Illustrated Encyclopedia of the Uniforms of the Roman World* (Lorenz Books, 2012)
Matthews, K.D., *The Early Romans: Farmers to Empire Builders* (McGraw-Hill Books, 1973)
Newark, T., *Ancient Celts* (Concord Publications, 2007)
Salimbeni, A. and D'Amato, R., *The Carthaginians 6th–2nd Century BC* (Osprey Publishing, 2014)
Salmon, E.T., *Il Sannio e i Sanniti* (Einaudi, 1995)
Sekunda, N. and Northwood, S., *Early Roman Armies* (Osprey Publishing, 1995)
Sekunda, N., *Republican Roman Army 200–104 BC* (Osprey Publishing, 1996)
Sekunda, N., *Greek Hoplite 480–323 BC* (Osprey Publishing, 2000)
Wilcox, P., *Rome's Enemies (2): Gallic and British Celts* (Osprey Publishing, 1985)
Wise, T., *Armies of the Carthaginian Wars 265–146 BC* (Osprey Publishing, 1982)

The Re-enactors who Contributed to this Book

Antichi Popoli

L'Associazione Culturale 'Antichi Popoli' nasce nel 2002 dalla passione di alcuni ragazzi per la storia e la promozione del patrimonio culturale del territorio. L'associazione attualmente cura la ricostruzione storica di tre periodi: medievale (1289–1325), etrusco (VI–IV sec. a.C.) e celtico (III-I sec. a.C.). Assieme ai suoi anni di esperienza e ricerca, può vantare anche l'iscrizione ad alcuni enti quali l'elenco regionale delle associazioni di rievocazione storica della Regione Toscana e il C.E.R.S. Il periodo etrusco prende in considerazione anni decisivi per i Tirreni, in cui ebbero luogo grandi cambiamenti nella storia di questo popolo sia per avvenimenti importanti che per nuovi assetti politici e sociali. Il periodo celtico segue la storia della Gallia Cisalpina dalla sua nascita fino all'inesorabile occupazione romana.

Contacts:
E-mail: antichipopoli@gmail.com
Website: http://www.antichipopoli.it/

Athenea Prómakhos

Athenea Prómakhos was created in Saragossa, Spain, during 2004, having as its main objective that of recreating and making known the history and daily life of the ancient Greek warriors. The group was officially registered as a non-profit cultural association in April 2006. In Greek mythology, Athenea (Athena) was the goddess of wisdom, skill and arts; for this reason, together with Apollo, she was the religious entity who represented in the best possible way the national spirit of the ancient Greeks. Athena was also a warrior-goddess, having the term 'Prómakhos' ('warrior') among her most important attributes. Unlike the blind violence and thirst for blood that characterized the fighting style of her brother Mars, Athena's military performances were guided by great intelligence and she usually preferred peaceful solutions to war (at least when possible). The association derives its name from this peculiar faculty of Athena (i.e. 'Athena the warrior'). With the progress of time, Athenea Prómakhos has grown considerably and now comprises many members living in every corner of

Spain. The association has not only expanded from a numerical point of view, but also from a qualitative one. It has greatly augmented the number of topics covered by its activities: after years of research and practical experience, the group is now able to cover all general aspects of the ancient Greeks' daily life. This means that the activities performed by the association are not focused only on military aspects, but also on those that characterized the civil life of Greek communities. In addition, members of Athenea Prómakhos are now able to reconstruct the daily life of foreign communities that came into contact with the Greeks, either as allies or enemies. These had a great influence over the development of Greek civilization and their main features had a deep impact over the evolution of Greek culture across the centuries. All the activities of Athenea Prómakhos are based on accurate research and analysis of all the most important primary sources dating back to the Classical period, be they literary or archaeological. Our researches are supplemented by the methodical consultation of all scientific publications dedicated to the history and archaeology of Ancient Greece and by frequent visits to some of the world's most important museums dedicated to the Greek civilization. Thanks to all the above, members of the association have been able to develop a direct and evidence-based knowledge of the objects that they recreate. This is constantly enriched by participation in important historical and archaeological conferences, as well as by the frequent contacts that the association has with important historians and archaeologists of the Greek world. The main objective of Athenea Prómakhos is that of using a true 'philological' approach in all its re-enacting activities, in order to reproduce the materials/objects in the best possible way and to perform educational activities of top quality. All this is made without renouncing the original 'spirit' of historical re-enacting, which comprises important social aspects. Thanks to our research and activities, which have had great success over the years, we have been able to participate in important and prestigious events in various European countries. Among these we should mention participation in 'Tarraco Viva', 'Les Grands Jeux Romaines' of Nîmes, re-enacting events at Aquileia and the 2,500th anniversary of the Battle of Marathon in Greece. Athenea Prómakhos has also performed at some important museums and archaeological sites, like that of El Efebo in Agde, Saint-Romain-en-Gal, Loupian, Olbia and Ampurias. We are always open to any kind of collaboration aimed at the spreading of historical/archaeological knowledge related to Greek civilization.

Contacts:

E-mail: apromakhos@gmail.com

Website: www.atheneapromakhos.org

Facebook: https://www.facebook.com/groups/799282110120899/

Confraternita del Leone/Historia Viva

La 'Confraternita del Leone' è un'associazione culturale di ricostruzione storica, con l'obiettivo di studiare, rivivere e divulgare la storia lombarda, con particolare attenzione a quella di Brescia e delle popolazioni che l'hanno abitata nei secoli. Le ricerche dei nostri studiosi spaziano senza limiti nella ricca e complessa storia locale, concentrando l'aspetto rievocativo e didattico sui periodi dal IV al I secolo a.C. in cui furono protagonisti Reti, Celti e Romani, quindi sul secolo VIII dei Longobardi, sull'età dei Comuni e delle Signorie del XII e XIII secolo e infine sul XVII secolo e l'epoca dei Buli sotto la Repubblica di Venezia. La ricerca storica della *Confraternita del Leone* si articola su tre differenti e complementari piattaforme di studio, la cui finalità è raggiungere dei risultati di globalità analitica in grado di estrinsecare degli spaccati storici di corretta filologicità e, ove possibile, di assoluto realismo e scientificità: istituto di ricerca storica, laboratori di archeologia sperimentale e accademia di antiche arti marziali occidentali. Nel partecipare ad eventi storici la *Confraternita del Leone* allestisce un accampamento di circa 500 metri quadrati, dispone di vari antichi mestieri dimostrativi con artigiani all'opera tra cui il fabbro con la forgia, la tessitura a telaio, la macinazione di cereali, l'usbergaro, lo speziale, il cerusico, la zecca, il cambiavalute, il cacciatore, l'arcaio, lo scrivano, l'avvocato e il fabbricante di candele; in battaglia sono schierati arcieri, balestrieri, fanteria, ariete, trabucchi e mantelletti.

Contacts:
E-mail: confraternitadelleone@gmail.com
Website: http://www.confraternitaleone.com/

Historia Viva

Historia Viva è un istituto di ricerca storica e archeologia sperimentale che, mediante lo studio delle fonti e l'attività sul campo in sinergia con rievocatori e ricercatori storici, realizza eventi culturali, festival, mostre, rassegne e propone spaccati di vita quotidiana, marziale e civile, dal neolitico fino alla metà del secolo scorso. Gli eventi realizzati affiancano alla componente ricostruttiva di momenti del passato elementi musicali e di gastronomia coeva, che concorrono a introdurre il pubblico in una interazione sensoriale completa che dà al visitatore un arricchimento culturale attivo, non subìto esternamente ma vissuto interiormente. *Historia Viva* collabora con produzioni documentaristiche, cinematografiche e di pubblicazioni storiche per quel che concerne gli aspetti legati alla marzialità e la contestualizzazione dei periodi analizzati.

Contacts:
E-mail: hveventi@gmail.com
Website: https://historiaviva.info/

Contoutos Atrebates

Contoutos Atrebates was created at the end of 2015, with the ambitious objective of reconstructing the daily life of one of Gaul's most important Celtic tribes, the Atrebates, who lived in northern France around present-day Arras. The Atrebates were part of the Celtic communities living in Gallia Belgica, and their name meant 'colonists' in the Celtic language. After being defeated by Julius Caesar, these fierce warriors did not accept surrender and thus later joined the great Gallic Revolt of 52 BC against the Romans. After the Battle of Alesia, the surviving members of the Atrebates negotiated a truce with the Romans and were permitted to abandon Gaul in order to create a new settlement in southern Britannia. In southern Britain the Atrebates founded a new kingdom that remained an ally of Rome for several decades; around AD 40 their territories were invaded by the Catuvellauni, this event being the main *casus belli* for the Roman invasion of Britannia some years later. Contoutos Atrebates tries to reconstruct the costumes and weapons of the Atrebates people during the crucial period of the Gallic Wars, but also from previous periods: our activities also include the re-enactment of important aspects related to daily life of a Celtic community, such as cooking or producing artefacts. We are interested in any kind of collaboration dealing with Celtic re-enactment from a scientific point of view.

Contacts:

E-mail: ctatrebates@yahoo.fr

Website: https://www.facebook.com/contoutos.atrebate

G.A.S.A.C.

L'Associazione *G.A.S.A.C.* (Gruppo per l'Archeologia Sperimentale di Arte Celtica) da diversi lustri promuove la conoscenza e la valorizzazione della cultura e dell'arte del popolo celtico. Presidente e 'motore' dell'Associazione culturale *G.A.S.A.C.* è Giuseppe Stucchi, nato nel 1949 a Trezzo sull'Adda. L'artista, stimolato da una passione innata, tramite l'Archeologia Sperimentale ha generato una vasta raccolta di oggetti e tuttora dispone di un'ampia collezione di alcune centinaia di pezzi (di cui fanno parte oggetti in bronzo, ferro, rame, argento ed oro). Riproducendo spade, elmi, collari e "torques" tutti realizzati rispettando le antiche tecniche costruttive artigianali celtiche. Nella sua sperimentazione l'artista è accompagnato da collaboratori tecnici ed archeologi che lo aiutano e lo supportano nella ricerca, nella raccolta di documentazione e nella realizzazione di nuove opere. Gli incontri avuti, nel recente passato, con i più autorevoli esperti di celtismo hanno affinato il lavoro di ricerca facendo produrre manufatti di esclusiva esecuzione e di grande pregio. La finalità dell'Associazione *G.A.S.A.C.* è la divulgazione della cultura e della storia del popolo celtico nostro antenato e di far apprezzare il suo patrimonio di conoscenze nella sua specifica originalità. L'Associazione auspica che attraverso la divulgazione si possa arrivare alla conservazione culturale di questo grande tesoro rappresentato dalla cultura del popolo celtico. Pertanto essa si prefigge di raggiungere questo obiettivo attraverso l'Archeologia Sperimentale, tramite metodologie didattico/illustrative che stimolino il desiderio di conoscenza di tutti coloro che visitano le mostre culturali allestite dall'associazione.

Contacts:
Website: http://www.artecceltica.it/

Hetairoi e.V.

Hetairoi e.V. is an association of people who have taken interest in various aspects of ancient Greek life and culture. Our goal is to recreate as many aspects as possible of the lives of people in ancient Greece as well as in neighbouring cultures. Our chosen method is called 'Living History', a concept developed out of battle re-enactments. Contrary to re-enactments, Living History interpreters make use of the so-called 'third-person interpretation', where they wear recreated clothing and equipment, but remain available for the audience to answer any questions and explain their activities. Sometimes short historical scenes are re-enacted, usually narrated by a member of the group explaining what is happening to the audience. As of 2020 our members are able to show reconstructions from the early Classical era, around 500 BC, to the late Hellenistic period, around 100 BC. Because you can't fully understand a culture without studying its neighbours, we have also recreated historical impressions from the important Greek neighbours of Rome, Persia, southern Italy, Thrace and Scythia. It is very important that the reconstructed equipment and clothing are based on the historic originals as closely as possible. We strive to base our recreations on the latest scientific research and invest a lot of time in research before starting our work. If we can't craft the pieces ourselves, our reconstructed equipment is sometimes created by craftsmen who are specialized in reconstructions for museums. The Hetairoi are at your service for events in museums or educational institutions, or other events where the transfer of knowledge is the main focus. As such we have already collaborated with, among others, museums like the Ephesos Museum and the Kunsthistorisches Museum in Vienna, the Reiss-Engelhorn-Museen in Mannheim, the Varusschlacht Museum und Park Kalkriese and the Historisches Museum der Pfalz in Speyer.

Contacts:
E-mail: info@hetairoi.de

Website: http://hetairoi.de

Facebook: https://www.facebook.com/Hetairoi.de

Les Ambiani

The Ambiani is a French association gathering enthusiasts of the Celtic Period. Composed of professional archaeologists and amateur historians, the association re-enacts a group of warriors and artisans from the Gallic Wars period (which took place around the mid-first century BC). The Ambiani were a Celtic tribe that inhabited the valley of the Somme in Gallia Belgica, nowadays in Picardy (in northern France). Our reconstructions are based on the most recent discoveries and try, as much as possible, to focus on the material culture of the people of the region of Amiens from where the association takes its name. Our activities include animations in the form of educational workshops (presentation of weapons and training of the infantry and cavalry, fighting in duels and in battle formations, religious ceremonies) and in workshops showing a series of activities, from the domestic sphere to more specialized craft productions (cooking, pottery, bone work, weaving, forging, minting coins). The Ambiani group works in collaboration with many specialists to develop and improve reconstructions, in order to follow the evolution of research and conduct experiments. We also created a small archaeo-site in Pont-Rémy, near Abbeville, with buildings based on archaeological discoveries, and have conducted an ambitious project involving the reconstruction of a Gallo-Roman barge.

Contacts:
E–mail: secretariat@les-ambiani.fr
Website: http://www.les-ambiani.com/
Facebook: https://www.facebook.com/Les-Ambiani-729215287167804/

Les Mediomatrici

In 2009, Thierry Chataigneau founded the Celtic Iron Age historical re-enactment group Mediomatrici with Cédric Mangin (vice-president), Jean-Marc Hein (treasurer) and Denis Aubry (secretary) in Alsace (France). The name Mediomatrici has been chosen to commemorate this real historical people living in Alsace 2,000 years ago. The Mediomatrici is an association dedicated to the La Tène Period; its main objective is presenting to the public the way of life of the Gauls during the first century BC. The Mediomatrici are dedicated to experimental archaeology, which allowed them to publish two studies (one devoted to Celtic helmets of the 'Novo Mesto type' and the other to the Gallic harvester 'Vallus') in the French magazine *Histoire Antique et Médiévale* by Editions Faton. The Mediomatrici present the combat techniques and Gallic armament of the final La Tène Period to the public during historical events, in archaeological museums and in schools (in France but also in other countries). We also present Gallic crafts: dyeing, weaving, leather work and fabrication of chainmail. As an example of experimental archaeology, the paintings on the shields of the Mediomatrici warriors have been realized with self-made milk painting containing natural pigments. The motifs painted on the shields are taken from illustrations reproduced on Celtic Iron Age coins. Thierry Chataigneau is currently publishing a historical Gallic soap-opera dedicated to the Mediomatrici during the Gallic Wars, for the magazine *Histoire de l'Antiquité à nos Jours* by Editions Faton. The group has already participated in many documentaries devoted to the Gauls and their history.

Contacts:
Website: http://mediomatrici.gaulois.over-blog.com and http://mediomatrici-gaulois. eklablog.com

Facebook: https://www.facebook.com/Mediomatrici and https://www.facebook.com/ durnacos.nertomari

Les Trimatrici

The proto-historic re-enactment troupe Trimatrici is attached to the MJC of Gerstheim in Bas-Rhin (France). Today it includes more than thirty people: archaeologists, craftsmen, students and simple amateurs. These are strongly linked together by a common interest in Gallic civilization and a desire to present it in the liveliest way possible. With this in mind, we try to reconstruct as faithfully as possible the craftsmanship, weapons and tactics of combat of Celts; more generally, we aim to create a reconstruction of Gallic life as it was near the end of Celtic independence (more specifically during the period of the Gallic Wars). The name of our association derives from the Médiomatrici and Triboci, two extremely important Celtic tribes of Gaul. Our services are modulated according to the circumstances (such as presentations in schools or in archaeo-sites), but we usually install a camp in which the public can follow the various workshops that we propose. These include craft activities, as well as the presentation of Gallic armour from the La Tène Period. Following our experiments in combat techniques, we offer demonstrations at various times of the day that are fun and educational. We operate throughout France and abroad, depending on our availability.

Contacts:
Website: http://trimatrici.fr/
Facebook: https://www.facebook.com/trimatrici

Teuta Arverni

The Teuta Arverni, formed according to the French Association Law 1901, brings together women, men and children who are all passionate about Celtic history. Thanks to historical evocation and scientific reconstruction, we present the life of the Arverne people in the first century BC, and especially during the Gallic Wars that opposed many Celtic tribes to the Roman legions of Julius Caesar. In particular, we recreate the following components of the Celtic world: the aristocracy and the military; the civil world, with particular attention to artisans and peasants; the daily life of a tribal community (including cooking, hygiene and education). Our works and reflections are based on discoveries made on the '*oppida*' and major sites of the Arvernes (Corent, Gergovie, Gondola, Aulnat-Gandaillat), but also on the writings of ancient authors and the most recent researches published by historians and archaeologists. Broadly speaking, the Teuta Arverni wish to reconstruct the Celtic world with an innovative approach that is much more in line with recent scientific and archaeological data, by correcting a number of clichés and received ideas that are still largely maintained by the media.

Contacts:
Website: http://www.teuta-arverni.com/

Teuta Osismi

Teuta Osismi is a historical re-enactment association, born in 2009, which aims to show how the Osismi people lived between the third and first century BC. It focuses on both military and civil life. The Osismi were a Celtic tribe living in the western half of modern Brittany and belonged to the so-called Armorican Confederation (known in the Celtic language as 'the country that faces the Ocean'). Our association mostly aims to democratize history and archaeology: for this purpose, we participate in events organized by museums and local institutions. These performances are mostly made in camps, with about twenty people including craftsmen and women but also a dozen warriors. Our camp is divided into workshops, each one showing a different kind of artisan work. Teuta Osismi has also contributed to many cultural events, such as movies about the Vénètes, short films and picture exhibitions with a historical perspective. The association also offers many animations for children, adults and elders. These include reconstructions of daily life in a Gallic camp, demonstrations of object-crafting with antique methods, initiations to some workshops (weaving, forge, leather, jewels, cooking), simulations of martial formations and demonstrations with our members. Our members gather each month to experiment new scientific hypotheses on Gallic fighting, by using different weapons according to their technical characteristics. Furthermore, we cooperate with Aremorica, another well-known association, working on crafts from the proto-historical period to the Gallo-Roman one.

Contacts:

Email: teutaosismi@gmail.com

Website: http://www.osismi.fr/

Facebook: https://www.facebook.com/teutaosismi/